GROUND STUDIES FOR PILOTS
Volume 2

By the same authors:

Ground Studies for Pilots, third edition
Volume 1, Radio Aids
Volume 3, Navigation General

Aviation Law for Pilots, third edition

By H. A. Parmar:

Navigation General and Instruments
(published by H. & J. Parmar)

GROUND STUDIES FOR PILOTS

Third Edition

Volume 2

PLOTTING AND FLIGHT PLANNING

S. E. T. Taylor
formerly British Airways and Chief Ground
Instructor, Malaysia Air Training, Kuala Lumpur;
Chief Ground Instructor, London School of Flying

H. A. Parmar
Senior Tutor, Bristow Helicopters Ltd
formerly Chief Ground Instructor, Malaysia Air Training, Kuala Lumpur;
Specialist Instructor, London School of Flying

GRANADA
London Toronto Sydney New York

Granada Publishing Limited – Technical Books Division
Frogmore, St Albans, Herts AL2 2NF
and
3 Upper James Street, London W1R 4BP
866 United Nations Plaza, New York, NY 10017, USA
117 York Street, Sydney, NSW 2000, Australia
100 Skyway Avenue, Rexdale, Ontario, M9W 3A6, Canada
61 Beach Road, Auckland, New Zealand

ISBN 0 246 11176 3

First published in Great Britain by Crosby Lockwood & Son Ltd 1970
Reprinted 1972
Second edition 1974, reprinted 1976, 1978
Third edition, in three volumes, 1979
Reprinted 1981 by Granada Publishing

British Library Cataloguing in Publication Data
Taylor, Sydney Ernest Thomas
 Ground studies for pilots. – 3rd ed.
 Vol. 2: Plotting and flight planning
 1. Airplanes – Piloting
 I. Title   II. Parmar, Hasmukhlal Amritlal
 629.132′5216   TL710

Text set in 10/12 pt IBM Press Roman, printed and bound
in Great Britain at The Pitman Press, Bath

Granada ®
Granada Publishing ®

Contents

Preface

The text of *Ground Studies for Pilots* has been completely revised and brought up-to-date: it is now produced in three volumes:

Vol. 1   Radio Aids
Vol. 2   Plotting and Flight Planning
Vol. 3   Navigation General

All matter for the Commercial and Airline Transport Licences is covered, but the problem of inter-relationship remains: frequent reference from one section to another and occasional simultaneous reading will be needed.

We have added further exercises which are typical of the present vogue, but again we must stress that speed with accuracy is an essential ingredient of the ground examinations, so continual timed practice from recent exam papers is quite vital. These are obtainable from CAA, 37 Gratton Road, Cheltenham.

The portions of Aerad charts are reproduced by kind permission of British Airways.

January 1979   S. E. T. Taylor
                                                         H. A. Parmar

Section 1

THE EARTH

1: Form of the Earth

The Earth

The Earth is not a true sphere but is flattened slightly at the poles. The more correct description of its shape may be an ellipsoid. Its Equatorial diameter of 6 884 nm exceeds its Polar diameter by about 23 nm. This flattening is known as Compression, which is merely the ratio of the difference between the two diameters to the larger diameter. Expressed in mathematical terms:

$$\text{Compression} = \frac{\text{equatorial diameter} - \text{polar diameter}}{\text{equatorial diameter}}$$

and its value approximates $\frac{1}{300}$. However, for our purposes, the Earth is a sphere.

Great Circle (G/C)

We all agree that a line which directly joins any two places on the Earth represents the shortest distance between them. Now, if we continue one end of this line in the same direction right round the Earth until it finally joins up at the other end, we find that the circle we have drawn just divides the Earth into two equal halves. Try it on an orange, keeping the knife blade at 90° to the skin. Putting the story in reverse we can state that the smaller arc of a great circle always represents the shortest distance between two places. This is all important from our point of view.

To define it, a Great Circle is a circle on the surface of the sphere whose centre is the centre of the Earth, whose radius is the radius of the Earth and which divides the Earth into two equal parts. Rather a lengthy one to learn, but know it and keep it in mind when dealing with Great Circle problems. The definition in fact tells us more about the nature of a great circle than just its contents:

(1) that only one Great Circle could be drawn through any two places — try again on an orange;

(b) but if those two places were diametrically opposite an infinite number of Great Circles could be drawn. Lines joining the two Poles are examples.

The Equator and all the lines of meridians (longitudes) are examples of Great Circles (although, technically, meridians are semi-great Circles).

Small Circle

A Small Circle stands in contrast to a Great Circle. By definition, any circle on the surface of the Earth whose centre and radius are not those of the sphere itself is a Small Circle. All latitudes (except the Equator) are Small Circles. They do not represent the shortest distance between two places.

Latitude and Longitude

A reference system in international use of which you have no doubt heard. First of all, a Great Circle is drawn round the Earth through the North and South Poles passing through Greenwich. That half of the Great Circle between the two Poles which passes through Greenwich is called the Prime or Greenwich Meridian. The other half is called the anti-Greenwich Meridian. The Greenwich meridian is labelled 0° and its anti-meridian, 180°. Thus, with this E − W division established, more Great Circles in the form of meridians could be drawn, both to the east of Greenwich and to the west.

The next step is to have a datum point for N − S divisions. This is obtained by dividing the Earth by a Great Circle mid-way between the two Poles, all points on it being equidistant from the Poles. Such a Great Circle, to your surprise, is called the Equator, and labelled 0° Latitude. Small Circles are now drawn, parallel to the Equator, towards both poles − these are parallels of latitude.

Definition of Latitude: it is the arc of a meridian intercepted between the Equator and the reference point. It is measured in degrees, minutes and seconds, and is termed North or South according to whether the place is to the north or south of the Equator.

Definition of Longitude: longitude is the shorter arc of the Equator intercepted between the Greenwich meridian and the reference point. It is measured east or west of the Prime meridian in degrees, minutes and seconds.

It is the meridians themselves that indicate North − South direction: the parallels run East − West.

The whole network of Latitude and Longitude (also called parallels and meridians) imagined to cover the Earth is called a Graticule. Thus, on a complete graticule we would see meridians starting from Greenwich as 0° going right round to the East and West up to 179°59′59″E and 179°59′59″W. 180° is common. Similarly to N − S, we would have parallels right up to 90°N and S, the Poles. A degree is divided into 60 minutes, and each minute is divided into 60 seconds (1° = 60′; 1′ = 60″).

And while on the subject of latitudes and longitudes, there are two more definitions you ought to be familiar with. They are: Change of Longitude and Change of Latitude.

Change of Longitude: it is the smaller arc of the Equator intercepted between the meridians of the reference points. It is named East or West according to the direction of the change.

Change of Latitude: it is the arc of the meridian intercepted between the parallels of the two places and is named North or South according to the direction of the change.

In the following sketch, if the flight was made from A to B, the ch long (change of longitude) is 2°E; ch lat (change of latitude) is 5°N. If the flight was from B to A, the ch long is 2°W and ch lat 5°S.

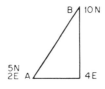

Fig. 1.1

Rhumb Line (R/L)

We established above that the shortest distance between any two places is along the Great Circle. This would be the ideal line (call it a 'Track') to fly. However, there is this disadvantage: the Great Circle from one point to another will cross the converging meridians at different angles. Since the meridians form the basis of our track angle measurements, this would mean continuous alterations to the track angles as the flight progresses.

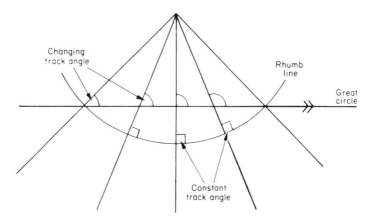

Fig. 1.2

Now, if a line joining the points was drawn such that it crossed each meridian at a constant angle, it must be a curve, not the shortest distance, but most convenient to follow, since alterations would not be forced on the aircraft simply to relate its direction to True North across the converging meridians on its route. Such a line is called a Rhumb Line. Definition: a Rhumb Line is a regularly curved line which cuts all the meridians at a constant angle.

Note these points:
(a) An aircraft flying a constant track is following a Rhumb Line track. This means that it is not doing the shortest distance.
(b) On the Earth, the meridians and the Equator are the only examples of Great Circles which are also Rhumb Lines.
(c) Parallels of latitude are rhumb lines.

Distances on the Earth's Surface

There are three different standards of measurements — nautical mile (nm), statute mile (sm) and kilometre (km).

A nautical mile is the distance on the surface of the Earth which subtends an angle of one minute of arc at the centre of the Earth. One minute of latitude is one nautical mile, average distance of 6 080 feet, that is, when measured up a meridian. One minute of arc along a Great Circle is one nm, and therefore, one minute of longitude on the Equator is one nm. But a minute of longitude measured along any other parallel will not be a nautical mile, since parallels are Small Circles, and the meridians converge towards the Poles where they all meet absolutely.

A statute mile is 5 280 feet and is used by motorists and jockeys. A kilometre is $\frac{1}{10\,000}$ of the distance from either Pole to the Equator, 3 280 feet, and is becoming increasingly used world-wide for meteorological distances.

Finally, on this quick run over of the elementary stuff known to all except those who suffered from a classical education ('Caesar was 2 milia passuum from the cohorts of Balbus') the conversion from one to another is on the circular slide rule on the computer; and on a map or chart, a distance on the dividers taken to the latitude scale, up and down the meridians, will give the distance in nautical miles, with reservations. Apart from the above, the following are useful figures to remember:

$$100 \text{ nm} = 185 \text{ km}$$
$$66 \text{ nm} = 76 \text{ sm}$$
$$1 \text{ inch} = 2\cdot54 \text{ cm}$$

NAVIGATIONAL PLOTTING

2: Theory and Practice of Plotting

If you wish to fly from one place to another, the first step is to join these places on the topographical map, marking this line with two arrows to show the direction of flight. This is your Track, and since it refers entirely to movement over the Earth's surface, the speed you go along a Track is not unnaturally called Ground Speed.

In flying, the wind speed, and the direction from which it blows, will affect the aircraft's movement: speed from a given direction being defined as velocity, the Wind Velocity will affect the aircraft's speed as well as Drift it from the direction to which its nose is pointing. Thus, if an aircraft has an Airspeed, and is set on a Heading, the W/V will act on it, resulting in a Track and Ground Speed.

Say your destination is due North of the departure point: the Track is 000° or 360°, angles always being measured from 000° all the way round to 000°, or 360° again; due East is 090°, due South 180°, and so on, always measured to the nearest degree. A wind from the West will clearly blow the aircraft off its Northerly Heading towards the East: so to keep on a Northerly Track would mean heading the aircraft to the West of North, the amount depending on the wind speed and the aircraft speed. This amount, measured from the Heading, is called the Drift.

The exact solution of this triangle of Velocities:

> Heading and Airspeed
> Wind direction and Wind Speed
> Track and Ground Speed

is of vital importance to the pilot. Knowing any four of the six ingredients, he can readily find the other two. We will do it from the basic triangle first, addressing ourselves to the problem as it faces a pilot preparing for a flight from:

> NORTHAMPTON (SYWELL)   5218N 0047W
>   to
> CARLISLE (CROSBY)   5456N 0248W

Remark how place names are always in capitals, and the ° and ′ signs are usually omitted when written by hand to avoid misinterpretation or ambiguity.

The Track is 335 True, True because we are referring to the True North Pole, and the protractor has been set on the chart with the True North arrow pointing precisely up the meridian through SYWELL. The Met man tells us that the W/V at the height we wish to fly is 270/40, i.e. the wind is blowing <u>from</u> due West at a speed of 40 knots (we always work in knots, nautical miles per hour). The aircraft we are using has a True Airspeed of 120 kt — more about the True bit later — irrespective of any forces acting on it, its speed through the air is 120 kt. We can now construct a Triangle of Velocities, to some suitable scale to find the two unknowns — the Heading of the aircraft, and its Ground Speed:

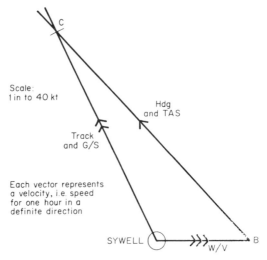

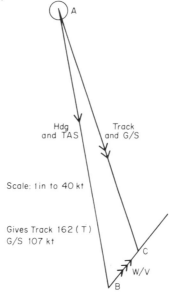

Fig. 2.1

Lay in the Track of 335. Lay in the Wind from 270, for 40 kt to B. With Centre B, and radius 120 kt, i.e. 3 inches strike an arc on the Track at C. Join BC.

BC is the Heading True of the aircraft – 318.

SYWELL to C measures 98 kt to scale – the G/S. All done – and note the arrows for Wind direction (3 of them) for Heading (1) and these two sets follow each other always.

That is the pre-flight case. Now consider a situation in flight, where the aircraft's heading is known, its True Airspeed is known, the W/V is known, and an idea of its Track and G/S is required: Heading 170(T) TAS 120 kt, W/V 220/20 – the terminology is self-explanatory.

Fig. 2.2

Or another case, in flight, with the aircraft on a definite Heading at its TAS, finds its Track and G/S by the pilot's skilful map reading and facile calculations: Heading 083(T), TAS 120 kt, Track 098, G/S 130 kt, what's the W/V?

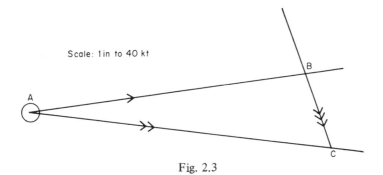

Fig. 2.3

The W/V is 342/35, and the pilot now has an up to date W/V for immediate use.

All these problems are done to vector scale, and the solution to any problem can readily be found, e.g. for a given TAS and W/V, state and show by means of a diagram, whether the greater drift will be experienced when wind direction is at right angles to Track, or at right angles to Heading.

Assume:
(a) TAS 120 kt, W/V 240/40 Hdg 330(T)
(b) TAS 120 kt, W/V 240/40 Track 330(T)

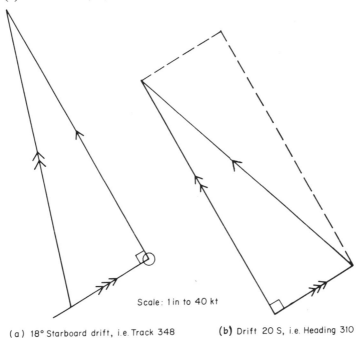

(a) 18° Starboard drift, i.e. Track 348   (b) Drift 20 S, i.e. Heading 310

Fig. 2.4

The drift is to starboard (that is, to the right of Heading) in each case. Greater drift is experienced when the W/V is at right angles to Track. In this case, the aircraft has had to turn its nose into the wind in order to maintain the required Track; in so doing, the G/S is reduced, thereby contributing to an increased drift. But in the second case with the W/V at right angles to Heading, the aircraft is simply being blown on to a Track which is not necessarily the required one. The difference in drift between the two cases is quite small.

It is commonplace to compare G/S with TAS by referring to a Headwind or a Tailwind component, always applied to the TAS. In (a) above, TAS 120 kt, G/S 127 kt, the tailwind component is 7 kt. In (b) above, a G/S of 113 kt gives a Headwind comp of 7 kt.

A further example:

When flying along a Track of 090(T), the drift is 16°S, and the wind component (i.e. difference between TAS and G/S) is zero.

(a)   What is wind direction?

(b)   Estimate TAS if wind strength is 80 kt.

Proceed as follows:

Draw from a point A the Track 090(T)

Drift is 16S, Heading must be 074(T)

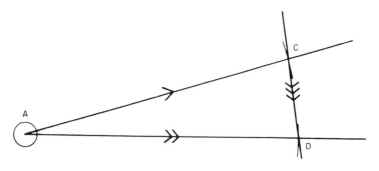

Fig. 2.5

With centre A and any convenient radius, strike off arcs C and D,
i.e. TAS = G/S = zero wind component.

Join CD and measure wind direction 350(T), and check the rules that Hdg and wind arrows follow each other.

Measure CD. That distance = 80 kt and say it is actually $\frac{7}{8}$ in. Return to vector scale. Measure AC, say $3\frac{1}{8}$ in = TAS.

Thus, by simple arithmetic:

$$\tfrac{25}{8} \div \tfrac{7}{8} \times 80 = 286 \text{ kt} = \text{TAS}$$

Once you settle down to flying for an airline, it is highly unlikely you will ever consider the triangle of velocities again: the solution to all the problems associated with it is done rapidly on the navigational computer, on the reverse of which is a circular slide rule which copes at once with times, speeds, distances, conversions, TAS, altitudes. You've bought one — if not, get cracking now — and be sure you have the explanatory tables that go with it. And to start with, why not check the above examples on the computer now?

Chart Work

You can now proceed to navigate on a suitable chart: the hoary old favourite is the Mercator chart, on which the latitude and longitude lines are straight lines at right angles to each other. This is now going out in the aviation world, and is not used in the Plotting exam for the Commercial Pilots' licence anyway: but for the exercise of grasping the elementary principles of navigation plotting, it is a simple chart to use. So if you are going for the CPL, work up to the paragraph on Radio Position Lines, and then press on to the detail of the Lambert Conformal: you will not be wasting your time, as the Mercator and its properties are still in the Navigation General Syllabus, and ATPL plotting is still on Mercator. You will need a GSGS 5158 now, and with your navigation tools at the ready, away we go.

Briefly, unlike the meridians on the Earth, which are semi-great circles meeting at the Poles (a Great Circle is a circle on the Earth's surface whose plane passes through the Earth's centre), the meridians on the Mercator appear as straight lines parallel to, and equidistant from each other. Unlike the parallels on the Earth, which are Small Circles whose planes are parallel to the plane of the Equator, the parallels on the Mercator appear as straight lines, parallel to each other all right, but increasing in distance apart towards the Poles.

This is the penalty for trying to spread part of a spherical surface into a workable plane surface. The full story is in the companion volume 3 'Navigation General', but for the creative activity you are about to embark on, mark the following important properties:

(i) A straight line drawn anywhere on the chart cuts all meridians at the same angle.

(ii) One minute (1') of latitude, up the side, represents one nautical <u>mile in that area</u>. Take your dividers, set them up the side or Latitude Scale between 5210N and 5240N. That represents 30 nm in the area roughly 5200N and 5300N. Keep that divider distance, and set one point on 5500N: up the scale it shows 28 nm. So you must always measure distance in the mean area of the line you are dealing with.

(iii) The longitude scale is constant, and measures longitude East or West of the Greenwich meridian <u>and that's all</u>.

So, if an aircraft is to go from WATTISHAM to MANCHESTER:

WATTISHAM   is Lat   5208N (of the Equator)
                      Long   0057E (of the Greenwich Meridian)
MANCHESTER   is Lat   5320N
                      Long 0216W

Plot in the places carefully on the chart, using a protractor for precision: circle each point, the symbol for a Fix (a known position), and join them up, putting the two arrows on the line, about a third of the way along, to indicate the Track you wish to follow over the Earth's surface.

To measure the Track Angle

Slap the centre of the protractor exactly over the point of WATTISHAM, with the North pointer due North, and the grid of the protractor exactly lined up with the grid of the chart. The Track measures 302(T) and never try to read half degrees.

To measure the distance

The latitude scale will be used, at about the mid-part of the Track. A satisfactory span here would be from 5230N to 5300N, representing 30 nautical miles; having selected this, you must keep to it for the whole Track: do *not* try to be terribly clever and measure the odd bit over at say 5210N. Take the mean 30 nm span, move it over the Track from WATTISHAM to MANCHESTER – 4 times and a bit over: the bit measured at 5230N is 18 nm.

The distance then is 138 nm.

To find the Estimated Flight Time

On the circular slide rule, at a G/S of 330 kt, for example, the time to fly this distance (138 nm) would be 25 minutes. An elementary flight plan is on its way, but let's consolidate the fundamentals first. Plot the following positions, and in each case find the Track and distance.

    (i)   Posn A 5220N 0531W to Posn B 5517N 0531W
            (Track is 360(T), and the distance can be a simple subtraction of
            5220 from 5517 = 177 minutes of latitude = 177 nm)
    (ii) Posn C 5410N 0450W to Posn D 5410N 0210W
            (Track is 090(T), and the distance will be taken from a 40 nm span
            covering 20 nm each side of 5410N = 95 nm)
        You put in the Track arrows, I suppose?
    (iii) Posn F 5451N 0502W to Posn G 5545N 0102E
            (Track is 075(T), distance 215 nm. Span here say 50 nm across the
            Track on the 0200W meridian)

Now to the circular slide rule: how long to fly each of these Tracks at a G/S of 280 kt? (38 minutes; 20 minutes; 46 minutes). And if in actual flight you did:

        A to B in 40 minutes
        C to D in 24 minutes
        F to G in 42 minutes

What was the actual G/S in each case? (265 kt, 237 kt, 306 kt).

The Tracks you have drawn are Rhumb lines, which cross each meridian at the same angle, easing the navigation of the trip. The shortest distance between any two points though is the Great circle, which appears on the Mercator chart as a curve concave to the Equator. We shall look into this matter fully ere long.

To find Heading and Ground Speed

Back to WATTISHAM – MANCHESTER, Track 302(T), distance 138 nm. Using a TAS of 240 kt, W/V 240/45, follow computer instructions to find the a/c's Heading and its G/S (292(T), 216 kt). The estimated flight time is solved as 38 minutes from the circular slide rule, and if one left WATTISHAM at 1215 hrs GMT (always work in GMT, even down under), the Estimated Time of Arrival, the ETA, is 1253 hrs.

Thus, the basic flight plan data for the trip is known, and we can soar into the air and navigate.

The Track is in already; at WATTISHAM, mark in the actual time of departure, the ATD, as 1217; plot in the a/c's True Heading 292(T), inserting the one arrow symbol. The Air Plot has been started, consisting of the Heading along which only

TAS can be measured; the Air Plot, the Heading, can only be started from a Fix, the name given to a position known for sure. This we have done.

Flying this Heading, we pass over PETERBOROUGH (5235N 0015W) at 1230 hrs precisely. Plot the position, as a small circled dot; it is a Pinpoint, the name given to a Fix obtained by visual observation of the ground; append the time 1230 to the symbol.

Now a Fix is wasted unless it is used to find some current information for the purpose of the flight; the uses are various, such as to find the W/V, check the G/S, amend the ETA, restart the Air plot (i.e. plotting the Heading one is on at that time from the Fix so that all information found henceforth is up to date), alter Heading to keep to the required Track to destination, and so on.

We will proceed first to find the W/V; there are two methods.

Method 1: To find the W/V by Track and G/S

The Heading and TAS we know to be 292(T), 240 kt. The Track we have made good, the TMG, is still 302, i.e. the drift is still 10S.

The distance from WATTISHAM to PETERBOROUGH is 51 nm, and this has taken 13 minutes, giving a G/S of 235 kt. So from the computer with this information, the wind is:

213/42 (Tr and G/S)

The method of solution is often put in brackets after the value, though it's in no way obligatory.

Method 2: To find the W/V by Air Plot

Measure along the Heading a distance of 52 nm flown in 13 minutes at a TAS of 240 kt, and mark with a '+' symbol for Air Position, with the time 1230.

Join the Air Position to the Fix for the same time 1230; this is the wind which has affected the a/c for the 13 minutes of flight.

Wind blows from air to ground in this horizontal relationship; this case measures 209(T), and the line is marked with 3 arrows pointing in the direction to which it is blowing. The distance is just over 9 nm, and since this effect has taken 13 minutes, the wind speed is 42 kt. We have then a W/V:

209/42 (Air Plot)

and the slight discrepancy from the previous solution arises from fractional differences; the protractor is not guaranteed accurate to $\frac{1}{2}^{\circ}$, and a W/V found over a period of less than 20 minutes magnifies small errors.

Having found the W/V, the next step is to put it to good use. The Fix is nicely on Track, yet the W/V found is different from forecast, so the Heading, G/S and ETA must be checked as a matter of routine.

Restart the Air Plot from the 1230 Fix, in other words plot in the Heading of 292(T). While the pinpointing, plotting and wind finding was going on, so was the aircraft; it is customary to plan alterations of Heading and its associated G/S, distance, time and ETA adjustments 6, 9, 12 or 15 minutes ahead of the Fix, depending on the speed of work and the time some Fixes take to obtain. These time intervals allow calculations to be done mentally, as they are simple proportions of an hour. The sample we are working on is but a few moments' task, so 6 minutes will suffice.

From the 1230 Fix, along the Heading just drawn, mark the Air Position at

1236, i.e. 24 nm (6 minutes at TAS 240 kt) in the accepted fashion. From this Air Position, lay off 6 minutes of W/V 209/42, i.e. 209/04.

This is the Dead Reckoning position, short for Deduced Reckoning, a term used by the sailor boys, I think: referred to as the DR Position, and the precise dot of the position enclosed by a triangle: where you think you are, or hope you are at 1236.

Join this DR Position to MANCHESTER: this is the new Track required. It happens to be 302(T) still, and the distance is 62 nm (measured, of course, with a span of 20 nm across the 5300N parallel).

On the computer then:

    Track 302(T)
    TAS 240 kt
    W/V 209/42

We find the Heading to steer will be 292(T), G/S 239 kt and on the slide rule, time $15\frac{1}{2}$ minutes, call it 16 minutes and ETA 1252. Check.

So although the G/S and ETA are the only changes, a comforting routine check of the progress of the trip has been made. Now plot in <u>from the 1236 Air Position</u> the Heading 292. From now on, the voyage is up to date as though it had all started <u>from the 1230 Fix.</u>

As a rider here, in actual flight, one would call this W/V 210/40. All winds are mean, they just do not blow for a period of time as a steady blast from a given direction.

Continuing our trip, tuning in to MANCHESTER on the Radio Compass, one can Home on without further worry. The *nose* of the aircraft on this instrument is 000, the tail 180, the exact starboard (right) beam 090, the exact port (left) beam 270, and so on. There is no reference to True North, or geographical direction, whatever, only a bearing relative to the aircraft's head. Thus, on MANCHESTER, nose 000, the $10°$ starboard drift we hope for will be proved by the needle pointing to 010 on the radio compass, steady, and all is well.

Your plot looks like this:

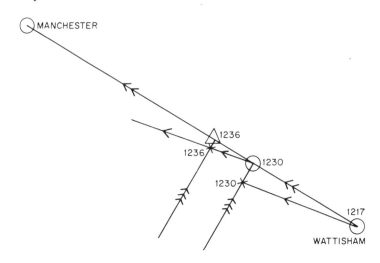

Fig. 2.6

Keeping an Air Plot going

Of course, one can fly a series of Headings, and keep a plot of them: the Air Plot must start or restart from a Fix, and all information required will relate in time from that Fix; all alterations of Heading will be from Air Positions.

Here's a practice run, the story on the right hand side: various accepted abbreviations are introduced, mostly self-evident, but all in the Glossary anyway.

0818 Posn A 5442N 0415W set Hdg 194(T)	20 min at 220 kt
TAS 220 kt	= 73 nm
0838 A/H 230(T)	7 min at 220 kt
0845 A/H 175(T)	= 26 nm
0850 PP 5313N 0430W	5 min at 220 kt
	= 18 nm
	Join Air Position to Fix
	W/D is 240
	W/E is 32 nm for
	32 min
(a) What mean W/V has been experienced?	∴ (a) 240/60
	Restart Air Plot at 0850 Fix
0901 A/H 088(T)	11 min along 175(T)
	at 220 kt = 40 nm
0911 A/H for Posn B 5345N 0010E	At 0901, plot 088(T)
	for 10 min at 220 kt
(b) What is DR Position at 0911?	= 37 nm
(c) Give Hdg(T) and ETA Posn B.	At 0911, lay off W/E
	for 21 min = 240/21
	∴ (b) 5245N 0255W
It all looks like this:	Join DR Posn to B.
	Track required 061(T)
	Distance 126 nm
	So with W/V 240/60,
	TAS 220 kt
	(c) Hdg 061(T)
	G/S 280 kt, time 27
	min ∴ ETA 0938

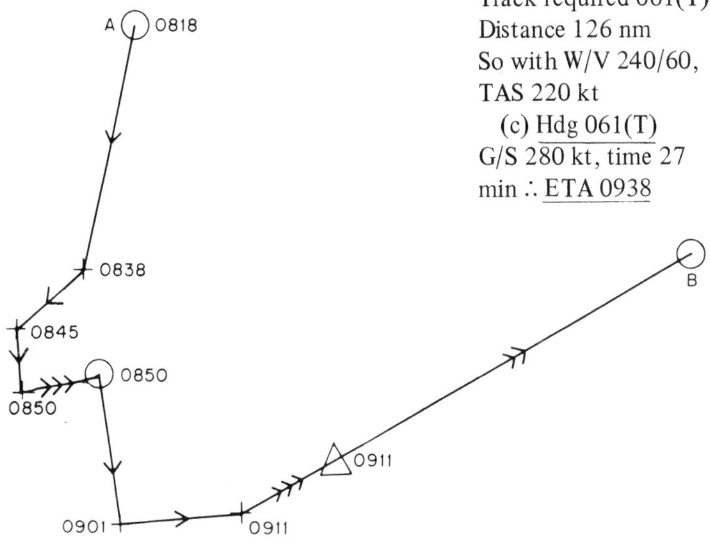

Fig. 2.7

Headings: True, Magnetic and Compass

A fuller story of these cheerful differences is given in the appropriate chapter in volume 3, but now consider them from a simple and practical viewpoint.

The True North Pole is a pointer for all plotting, the meridians of longitude converging there. The Magnetic Pole is some hundreds of miles from the True North, and it is the Magnetic North Pole which is of value to the airman, since a freely suspended magnet will point to it. This magnet is the compass needle, which is used in one form or another to indicate direction to the pilot in his aircraft, in the clear or cloud, by day or night.

To be brief, and to avoid the theory for the moment, at any spot on the Earth's surface, the Magnetic direction varies from the True, and this Variation is measured as a number of degrees E or W of the True North Pole, e.g., a perfect magnet, freely suspended, might point to a position $5°$W of the True North Pole. On the chart in front of you, you will find that all places of equal magnetic variation are joined by lines called Isogonals, and the value of the variation printed on each. You will notice that a date is also given, for the Magnetic Pole adds to the confusion by moving round the True North Pole in a clockwise direction at the rate of about one cycle every 960 years. The annual amount of the change of value of local variation is noted on the Chart in the bottom left hand corner, $7'$E. Thus, for a place where variation is '10W 1971' in 1980 the variation would be $9 \times 7'$E $= 1°03'$E, lessening the 10W variation by $1°$ to 9W for our purpose.

An additional complication for the pilot is the fact that he is using a sensitive compass needle housed in a metallic box of tricks called an aeroplane, chockful of electrical and radio gear, all of which affect his particular compass, and give it an error one side or the other of the Magnetic North. This error is called Deviation, and is labelled E or W of the <u>Magnetic</u> North Pole. Remember that it is the deviation of one particular compass in one particular aeroplane, and the deviation will have been found and recorded on a card beside the compass.

Examine Figs. 2.8 and 2.9.

And the rule:

Start at the compass, move towards Magnetic, thence to True, then W is minus, and E is plus.

The examples would read:

C	D	M	V	T
071	6W	065	15E	080
270	10W	260	20W	240

Cadbury's Dairy Milk Very Tasty. You fly Compass, you plot True.

True Airspeed (TAS), Rectified Airspeed (RAS), Indicated Airspeed (IAS)

The Airspeed on the dial of the instrument on the panel is the Indicated Airspeed: correct this for any error caused by the peculiarities of the aircraft or of the particular instrument itself (usually again from a card nearby, and the correction varies with speed), and we get the Rectified Airspeed.

Now the thing is ploughing through the air which is very very variable in density due to changing temperatures and pressures, and it cannot cope: so a correction must

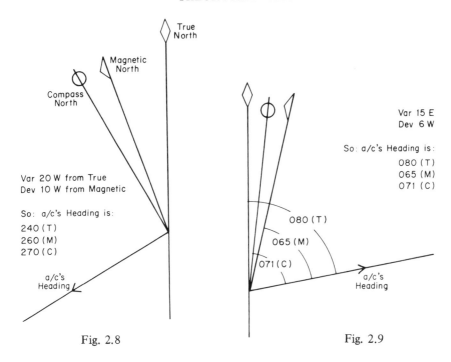

Fig. 2.8   Fig. 2.9

be made to allow as much as possible for the conditions the aircraft is flying in. This
is done from a window in the circular slide rule or from a graph in many modern
aeroplanes; this correction of height and temperature to RAS gives the TAS, the
actual speed the a/c is making through the air, of vital significance in navigation plotting, to say nothing of cruise control. An example or two:

    60 000 ft altitude, Temp $-60°C$, RAS 100 kt gives TAS 315 kt
    10 000 ft altitude, Temp $-10°C$, RAS 100 kt gives TAS 114 kt

Navigation on the Climb
Actually, this is mainly of academic interest: the pilot keeps an eye on the radio
instruments as a check, but the first real Fix is wanted on levelling-off, check the
level TAS, find after a little time the W/V, find out how the forecast wind compares
and so on. BUT, the wind blowing at expected levelling altitude will be different from
the mean W/V experienced on the climb, so the Heading to hold to keep to Track
must be flight-planned, and the first Fix obtained either on the way up or on levelling
off is of value only for checking position in relation to the Track required. A found
W/V would be very mean indeed, and pretty futile for navigational use. So keep the
Air Plot going, always, until good level fixes are obtained, and useful indicative W/Vs
can be found for use on the next leg, or part of a leg. And don't forget, however
sophisticated one's departure from an aerodrome using radio aids, though you may
be keeping to Track, constant checking is vital.

    The method is not at all difficult, and can be used before and in flight. As an
example, a climb from 1 000 to 17 000 ft gives a mean altitude of 9 000 ft; this is
found by adding the lower altitude to the upper and then dividing by 2, though
there's nothing to prevent the rational way of 17 000 − 1 000 = 16 000, divide by

2 = 8 000, and as the climb began at 1 000 ft, then the mean is 9 000 ft. Taking this mean altitude, where the Temp is say −10°C, and offering a constant climb RAS of 180 kt, the mean climb TAS is readily solved as 202 kt. This is quite adequate for the flight plan, and in flight too if required.

Try a plot question on the Mercator to clinch the deal, step by step:

0900 Posn 5217N 0528W S/H 013(T), 1 000 ft, climbing

    Forecast 2 000 ft W/V 250/35 Temp + 5°C
        5 000 ft W/V 265/50 Temp −1°C
        10 000 ft W/V 270/60 Temp −11°C
        15 000 ft W/V 285/60 Temp −21°C

    RAS 167 kt for the climb

0936 Level 13 000 ft, RAS 190 kt

    Give DR position at 0951.

The mean altitude is 7 000 ft, and the Temp at 7 000 ft is −5°C by interpolation; climb TAS is therefore 182 kt. Plot the Hdg 013(T) for 36 min at this TAS = 109 nm, and mark this Air position with symbol and time as usual. Solve the level TAS, 13 000 ft, RAS 190 kt, Temp −17°C = 227 kt

From the 0936 Air position, continue the Hdg 013(T) for 15 min at 227 kt = 57 nm, and mark it as 0951.

The W/Vs experienced so far are:

    36 min of climb W/V meaned at 7 000 ft 267/54
    15 min of level W/V at 13 000 ft   279/60

So at the 0951 Air position, plot the W/E for the climb 267/32 and from the end of this line, add the W/E for the period of level flight 279/15.

This is the DR position 5458N 0305W and the plot looks like this:

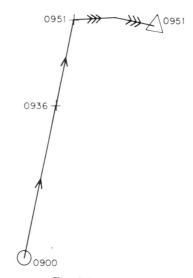

Fig. 2.10

Being of an enquiring mind, you will have asked yourself why not work out climb Track at climb G/S for 36 min, and level Track at level G/S for 15 min and arrive at once at the DR position. In a simple case like this, the answer will be correct, but the

Air Plot hasn't kept going, breaking the fundamental rule of plotting the known factors of Hdg and TAS at all times.

As you're in the mood, try this:

1230 Position A 5210N 0550W, Heading 350(T), 3 000 ft Temp −3°C
        climbing to 17 000 ft at a constant RAS 148 kt, mean W/V 320/30
1248 Level 17 000 ft, Temp −29°C, RAS 180 kt, W/V 290/45 A/H 050(T)
1308 A/H to return to Posn A
     (a)   Give the DR position at 1308
     (b)   What is Hdg(T) and ETA posn A?
Answer: (a)   5336N 0355W
           (b)   230(T), ETA 1340

Position Lines

Having mastered the elementary rules of plotting, it is necessary now to address ourselves to the problem of how to get a Fix. So far, we have been served only by Pinpoints, picked up by identifying a spot on the ground and transferring its Lat and Long to the chart.

A Position Line is the line on the chart, straight or curved, on which the aircraft is known to be, or to have been, at a particular time. Should an a/c cross a railway line, then its ground position is somewhere along the railway at the time of crossing; another bearing from some other location at the precise time of crossing would fix the a/c's position at the point of intersection of the two position lines.

The commonest way of obtaining a position line (P/L) is by radio compass. Bearing in mind that the nose of the a/c is 360°, an a/c tuned in to a radio station might read an angle of 283°, say, and this angle is relative to the a/c's Heading. If the relative bearing is added to the a/c's Heading, then the bearing from True North is found; the reciprocal, or 180° different, can be plotted from the station, whose position is of course known. Here's an example, with the face of the radio compass enlarged:

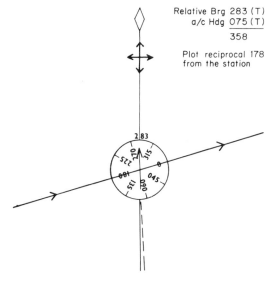

Relative Brg 283 (T)
a/c Hdg 075 (T)
358

Plot reciprocal 178
from the station

Fig. 2.11

Consider the case of an a/c passing North of a radio station on a Heading 270(T), making good or hoping to make good a Track of 260(T).

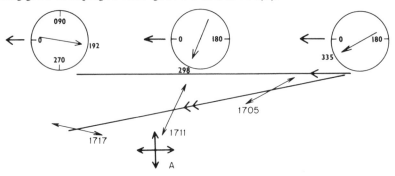

Fig. 2.12

1705 Bearing Relative of A 335
1711 Bearing Relative of A 298
1717 Bearing Relative of A 192

The bearings are relative to the nose of the aircraft, i.e. its Heading (T), and the working looks like this:

	1705	1711	1717	
Brg Rel	335	298	192	You can always
Hdg(T)	270	270	270	subtract 360 –
	605	568	462	you are only
	–360	–360	–360	going round the
Brg(T)	245	208	102	clock again.
Plot	065	Plot 028	Plot 282	

Imagine now that the radio station moves in the same direction at the same speed for the same time as the aircraft, i.e. at its Track and G/S, then the first two P/Ls could be placed at 1717, and the P/Ls would be transferred as though the station had stayed with the aircraft. Thus, the P/Ls are transferred along the Track to produce what is strangely enough called a Running Fix, with the P/Ls emanating from the same station abeam of the Track.

The example above would be calculated as follows for a G/S of say 200 kt
the 1705 P/L could be transferred for 12 minutes – 40 nm
the 1711 P/L could be transferred for 6 minutes – 20 nm
along the track. Where they all cross will give a Fix, and despite any incorrect assumptions about the track and G/S, the Fix will be reasonable if not perfect.

Thus

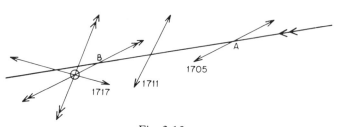

Fig. 2.13

A transferred P/L is symbolised by double-arrowed ends, and is untimed: the distance A 1705 to B 1717, the transfer point, is the 40 miles referred to, and the 1705 P/L is simply paralleled through this point with the protractor. The Fix at 1717 may not be so clear cut, and could have the following appearance.

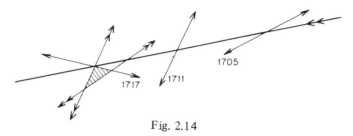

Fig. 2.14

The shaded area is called a Cocked Hat, and while it would cause some dubiety about its accuracy, it's better, far better, than no Fix at all. The centre of the cocked hat is taken as the Fix: theoretically bisect each angle of the triangle, and the intersection of the bisectors gives the Fix. In practice, point the Fix visually, but if it's a large cocked hat, don't call it a Fix but an MPP, a Most Probable Position, so that when a reliable accurate Fix does come along you know to what extent to pin your faith on W/V and G/S found.

A P/L that cuts Track at right angles, or very nearly so, can be used to check G/S, and that G/S used for the transfer of P/Ls at the time: you would have to be well off the Track you thought you were making good to have a really appreciable error.

A P/L that is parallel to the required Track indicates the distance off; and should you know the distance flown from the last Fix, the Track Made Good (TMG), can be fairly established.

A useful trick to find TMG if the a/c is passing a station from which position lines can be taken by any means whatsoever, is to plot them at agreeable time intervals and then place the long ruler across them so that the linear divisions are proportional to the times of observation: the line thus obtained is the TMG.

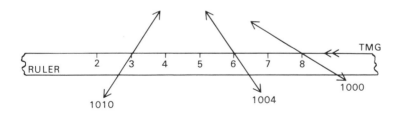

Fig. 2.15

Say 5 mm represents a minute of time. Then 1000 to 1004 is 2 cm, and 1004 to 1010 is 3 cm: the ruler adjusted at these intervals as shown in Fig. 2.15 will give the TMG.

A steady back-bearing from a departure point, or from a station which the aircraft has recently passed overhead, will indicate TMG, and in fact that is a common method of departure from aerodromes.

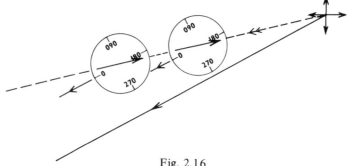

Fig. 2.16

All straightforward practical stuff. A P/L can be circular, such as the distance from a station registered on the Distance Measuring Equipment (DME) dial on the panel. To transfer one of these, transfer the origin at the same Track angle at the same G/S for the required time, and replot the P/L from the new centre viz:

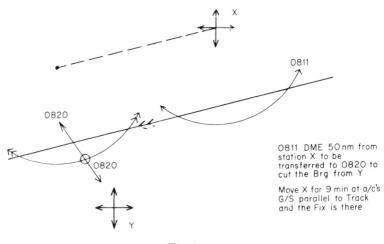

0811 DME 50 nm from station X to be transferred to 0820 to cut the Brg from Y

Move X for 9 min at a/c's G/S parallel to Track and the Fix is there

Fig. 2.17

Conditions will arise when a decision may have to be taken as to which part of the arc is the correct one; invariably the DR G/S will give the clue. Of course, it follows that a bearing and DME distance from the same station will give an instant fix.

Transferred P/Ls along the Air Plot

P/Ls can be transferred along the Air Plot when one does not know the Track or is highly suspicious of it, making the G/S a matter of guesswork. The topic is of academic interest, but sufficiently simple to be worth knowing. The odds against using it in the air are enormous.

Join 1022 Air Position to any point B to give a convenient vector of 22 units, the minutes flown since the last Fix. At Air Position 1029, parallel this line for 29 units to a point C. Transfer the P/L through C.

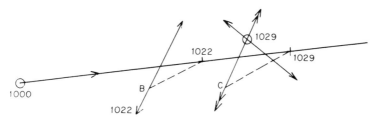

Fig. 2.18

It matters not at all which direction the 1022 vector is taken; the parallel at C to scale will give the correct transfer.

Radio Position Lines

This type is in constant use. They are often plotted on special charts which already have numbered series overlaid, so that having obtained a reading on a particular aid, it can be plotted at once by visual interpolation near the Track. Here for the moment we will concern ourselves with the simple types to be plotted on the Mercator chart before us.

Yet another problem now rears its head; all radio waves follow the shortest route over the Earth's surface, that is, they are Great Circles, and would appear on the Mercator as curves, impossible to plot. A G/C must be converted in consequence into a R/L, using a well-worn factor called the Conversion Angle.

Consider this example:

An a/c on Hdg 330(T) obtains a relative bearing of station A of 268. The measuring is done in the aircraft.

Brg Rel	268	
Hdg(T)	330	
	598	
	−360	
Brg(T)	238	G/C see diagram
CA	− 2	for example
Brg(T)	236	R/L
Plot	056	reciprocal from the station

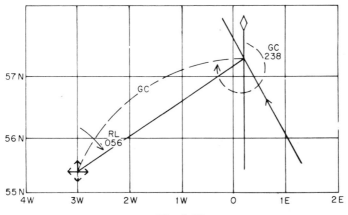

Fig. 2.19

It can be seen that:
    (i)   The work of measuring has been done in the a/c, the angle 268 relative, G/C.
    (ii)   The Rhumb Line bearing from True North must be less than the Great Circle
          bearing from True North.
    (iii) The conversion angle depends on the change of longitude between the a/c
          and the station at the time of taking the bearing.
$\frac{1}{2}°$ are ignored, and the CA can be read off the ABAC scale in the top corner of the
chart.

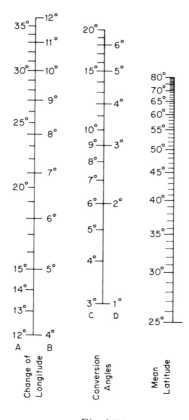

Fig. 2.20

Fig. 2.20 gives the operational ABAC scale as used in flying practice; if scale A is used
for change of longitude, read off CA on scale C; if scale B is used ditto read off CA on
scale D. A ruler is placed across. The ABAC scale solves graphically the formula for
conversion angle

      $CA = \frac{1}{2}$ ch long × sin mean lat

We've never known anyone carry log tables in the air, nor have we ever known
an airman who can roll off the sine of any angle from memory; it was different on
ships, perhaps, but on aeroplanes the time is rather short in which to work out the
stuff.
    A ch long of 0 will give a CA of 0, since the a/c is on the same meridian or so as
the station, and a meridian is both a G/C and a R/L.

Consider now an a/c taking a bearing on a station on the a/c's Easterly side:

Brg Rel	123
Hdg(T)	330
	453
	−360
Brg(T)	093 G/C
CA	+ 2 for example
Brg(T)	095 R/L
Plot	275 from the station

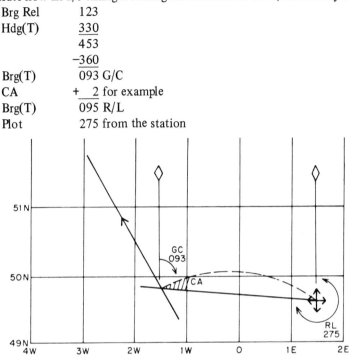

Fig. 2.21

The CA in this case is added; the rule is apply the CA towards 180, that is if the bearing is more than 180, subtract CA, add if less. The diagram will help in clarifying the rule, but always ask yourself who is doing the work and apply the CA to the angle measured. In the example, the angle of 093 was measured in the a/c, and this is the figure to convert; thence proceed to plot from the known station.

This is the rule in the Northern hemisphere. In the Southern, apply away from 180, subtracting if less than 180, adding if more.

Here is the same example down South, CA now −2, illustrated as follows:

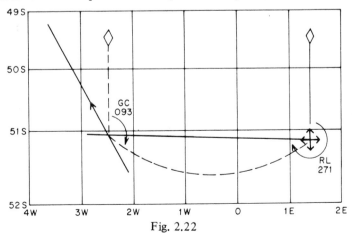

Fig. 2.22

Plotting radio bearings given by a station

A radio station can give you:

> QTE 'your bearing True from me is . . .'
> QDM 'your Hdg(M) to reach me with zero wind is . . .'
> QDR 'your bearing(M) from me is . . .'

These are the commonest ones, and the station can give them to an a/c either verbally on the R/T, or the signal can be picked up automatically and read off a dial on the panel. Remember though that the station has sent out the signal, and all the work of measurement has been done on the ground; no part of the work has been done in the a/c. So we must concern ourselves only with the station and the signal or bearing that emanated therefrom. To get the R/L bearing, we must get to the station first, get rid of the Variation, if applicable, which is noted there, and apply the CA to the G/C bearing from it.

For example: VOR gives QDM   244
                      Var   10W at the station
                      G/C   234(T) received in the a/c
                                       180
                      G/C   054 station sent out
                      CA   +   2 say
                      R/L   056 which plot

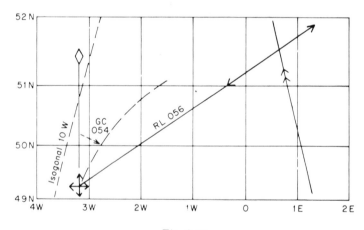

Fig. 2.23

It's the station that's done the work. The same rules about the application of CA towards 180 in the Northern hemisphere, away from 180 in the Southern, hold good, but get what the station measured True first.

RMI Bearings

VOR bearings on the RMI are QDMs, and are prepared for plotting as outlined above.

ADF bearings are still QDMs, but since they are computed as it were <u>within the aircraft</u>, deviation and variation at the aircraft must be extracted, and CA applied before plotting the reciprocal.

In both cases, plotting on the Mercator, the rules of conversion angle apply.

Try this little exercise:

0316 DR Position 5340N 0140W, Hdg 334(T), RAS 180 kt, flight level 8 500 ft,
     Temp −10°C, W/V 030/40

0326 NDB in position 5430N 0040E bears 101 relative

0331 VOR in position 5500N 0500W QDM 307

0337 NDB in position 5540N 0210W bears 043 relative
        Give the a/c's position at 0337.

Check your working, and flagellate yourself if you fell into any of the traps like
setting Hdg from a DR position, like not reading drift at once off your computer to
find the Track from a given Heading, with no fiddling.

    TAS 200 kt, Track 324(T), G/S 180 kt

0326			0331			0337	
Brg Rel	101		QDM	307		Brg Rel	043
Hdg(T)	334		Var	11W at the stn		Hdg(T)	334
	435			296(T)			377
	−360		Recip	116			−360
Brg(T)	075 G/C		CA	+ 1		Brg(T)	017 G/C
CA	+ 1		Plot	117		CA	0
Brg(T)	076 R/L					Brg(T)	017 R/L
Plot	256					Plot	197

    Transfer 0326 P/L for 11 min at G/S 180 = 33 nm

    Transfer 0331 P/L for 6 min at G/S 180 = 18 nm

The Fix at the crossing of the three P/Ls is 5432N 0246W

This method of setting out helps to check the point of application of CA; the
first and last bearings were actually measured in the aircraft, while the middle one
was a dial reading of a particular signal lined up at the station.

That's about it for plotting on the Mercator; here is a paper to work through to
consolidate the essentials.

Chart GSGS 1938, and use variation for the year of the chart.

Question 1

0910 Position A 5310N 0550W S/H 025(T), RAS 165 kt, F/L 12 000 ft,
    Temp −15°C. Forecast W/V 340/35. The following bearings are obtained from
    a station in position 5540N 0420W

          0955 QTE 151

          1003 QTE 123

          1011 QTE 095

  (a) Give the position at 1011.

  (b) What mean W/V has been experienced since 0910?

1017 A/H for Position B 5600N 0300E

    (c) What is DR position at 1017?

    (d) Give Hdg(M) and ETA position B. (Use mean Variation)

Question 2

1120 DR position 5450N 0220W, Hdg 026(T), TAS 180 kt,
    forecast W/V 320/45.

1123 NDB at position C 5330N 0100W bears 138 relative by radio compass.

1129 NDB in position B 5531N 0000 bears 047 relative by radio compass
    Give the position at 1129.

Question 3

1210 VOR position C 5330N 0100W S/H 005(T), TAS 180 kt. Subsequently VOR
    equipment tuned to C indicates a steady QDM 204
1240 VOR position D 5457N 0040E QDM 114
    What is W/V?

Question 4

1325 Position D 5457N 0040E S/H 160(M), 1 500 ft climbing to 11 500 ft at
    RAS 145 kt, mean Temp for climb 0°C, mean W/V for climb 230/25.
1345 Level 11 500 ft, Temp −11°C, RAS 160 kt, W/V 255/40 A/H 180(M)
    Give the DR position at 1405.

Question 5

1500 Position E 5200N 0100E S/H 290(M), TAS 180 kt, forecast W/V 050/30
1528 A/H 335(M)
1550 A/H 240(M)
    What is DR position at 1612?

Question 6

    Hdg 295(C), deviation 2W, variation 6E, RAS 150 kt, flight level 12 500 ft,
    Temp −10°C.
    The aircraft flies a distance of 260 km in 43 min making good a Track of 292(T).
    What is the W/V?

Answers

1   TAS 194 kt, Track 034(T), G/S 170 kt.
    Plot QTEs direct from station, CA 0 in each case.
    Transfer 0955 P/L for 16 min at G/S 170 kt = 45 nm.
    Transfer 1003 P/L for 8 min at G/S 170 kt = 22 nm
    (a) Fix 5536N 0255W
    TMG 035 ∴ drift 10S
    178 nm in 61 min = G/S 175 kt
    (b) 330/38 (Tr and G/S)
    Plot Hdg 025(T) from Fix for 6 min at TAS 194 kt = 19 nm
    Plot W/E 330/04
    (c) DR position 5550N 0238W
    Track required 087(T), distance 194 nm to B
    Hdg 077(T) = Hdg 085(M). G/S 208 kt, time 56 min
    (d) 085(M) ETA 1113

2   Track 041(T) G/S 167 kt

1123 Brg Rel 138		1129 Brg Rel 047	
Hdg(T)	026	Hdg(T)	026
Brg(T)	164	Brg(T)	073
CA	0	CA	0
	164		073
Plot	344	Plot	253

    Position at 1129 5517N 0125W

3   QDM 204 = 195(T) Plot 015(T) = TMG
    1240 QDM 114 = 106(T) Plot 286
    Drift 10S, distance gone 99 nm, G/S 198 kt
       W/V 252/39 (Tr and G/S)
4   Mean height on climb 6 500 ft, mean Temp 0°C gives climb TAS 158 kt 20 min
    on Hdg 152(T) = 53 nm
    Level TAS 187 kt for 20 min on Hdg 173(T) = 62 nm
    Lay off climb W/E 230/08
    From end of climb wind, lay off level W/E 255/13
       DR position at 1405 5316N 0206E
5   Airplot   Hdg   282(T) for 84 nm
                 Hdg   326(T) for 66 nm
                 Hdg   230(T) for 66 nm
    W/E for 1 h 12 min = 050/36
       DR position at 1612 5209N 0427W
6   295(C) = 293(M) = 299(T)
    TAS 180 kt, 260 km = 140 nm in 43 min = G/S 195 kt
    TMG 292(T) gives drift 7P
       W/V 060/28 (Tr and G/S)

3: Plotting on the Lambert Conformal

This chart is now invariably used in the air, and of course has its virtues balanced by consequent drawbacks; these are fully dealt with in volume 3 'Navigation General'; here we will use it practically.

Radio bearings are G/Cs, and straight lines drawn on a Lambert are G/Cs for all practical purposes, so we're on easy street at once. A G/C Track can be flown, and it's the shortest distance between two points. The snag is the meridians converge towards the nearer Pole, so that an angle measured at one meridian will be different from that angle measured at another for the same straight line by the amount the meridians converge. The value of this convergence is found from the formula:

Convergence = ch long x n

where n is the sine of that parallel of latitude on which the chart is constructed to make convergency constant over that particular sheet. This is noted in a corner of the chart as an actual figure. On the plotting charts specially prepared for the CPL examination, n is taken as 0.8, being the sine of the mid-parallel 52N, quite accurate enough to one place of decimals.

Before discussing the methods of allowing for convergence, examine the implications of the following diagram:

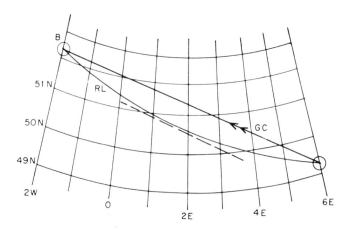

Fig. 3.1

1. The mean G/C Track would be measured at meridian 0200E.
2. As the R/L is concave to the nearer Pole, the tangent to this curve measured at 0200E would be the R/L Track.

3. The initial G/C Track would be measured at 0600E. On a long drag, clearly this
    would be required for a start, and if regular fixes are obtained at shortish intervals,
    new Tracks would be progressively measured at new meridians; adjust yourself to
    the mean meridian over the next leg to be covered.
4. Distance is measured on the latitude scale as usual. The scale of the chart is
    sufficiently correct for all practical purposes, so any part of the latitude scale will
    do.

To plot radio bearings
As always with radio bearings, ask yourself the question 'who is doing the work'?
Such bearings as QDM, QDR, QTE present no problem; they are sent out from a
station whose position is known, whose meridian is known, and it is there that the
measuring is being done, so convergence is no factor in their plotting. But where the
working and measuring are done in the aircraft at the aircraft's meridian, and the
plotting must then be done from the station's meridian, then convergence is in with a
bang; it must be applied.
    The simple case first:

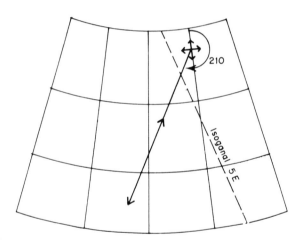

Fig. 3.2

Station gives QDM 025
            Var   5E at the station
            G/C 030(T)
    Plot 210 from the station, using his meridian.
And that's all.
    Now to measure a bearing in the aircraft and plot it from the station; the conver-
gence between the aircraft's DR position and the station must be considered. There
are two methods, and the first is the safer, easier and more practical. This is to
transfer your meridian to the station and measure from that.
    For example, an aircraft on Hdg 325(T) measures a relative bearing 100 from a
radio station. Proceed as follows:

Brg Rel 100
Hdg(T) 325
　　　　 425
　　　 −360
Brg(T)   065 G/C
Plot   245 from the transferred meridian

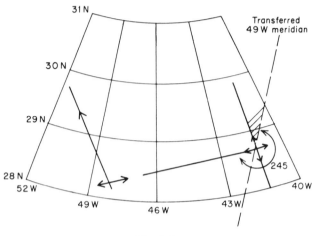

Fig. 3.3

The alternative method is to use the convergence formula
　　　　Convergence = ch long x n
In the above case 8 x 0·5 as n will be about sin 30
The working is:

Brg Rel 100
Hdg(T) 325
　　　　 425
　　　 −360
　　　　 065
Converg + 4
　　　　 069
Plot   249 from the station's meridian

The shaded angle on the diagram has been mathematically taken care of. The rule for application is the same as for conversion angle on the Mercator, towards 180, and throw it in before you extract the reciprocal to plot.

　　VOR readings on the RMI are QDMs, and the only requirement before plotting is to extract the variation at the station before plotting the reciprocal. But ADF bearings, QDMs withal, demand that deviation and variation at the aircraft are extracted and convergence applied before plotting the reciprocal, since the work has been done in the aircraft.

　　Here is an exercise, using Lambert 1:1000 000, the CPL exam chart:
1100 Position C 5545'N 0213E S/H 188(T), TAS 195 kt
1125 VOR C gives QDM 008
　　(a) What mean drift has been experienced since 1100?

1135 NDB in position 5400N 0200W bears 092 relative by radio compass
    (b) Give the position at 1135
    (c) What mean W/V has been experienced since 1100?

Answer
1125 QDM 008
    Var   <u> 7W</u> at C
          001(T)
    Plot   181(T) direct = TMG which gives <u>drift 7P</u>   (a)
1135 Brg Rel 092
    Hdg(T) <u>188</u>
    Brg(T) 280 G/C
    Plot   100 from the meridian 02E transferred to the station
    Alternatively Brg Rel 092
                Hdg(T) <u>188</u>
                Brg(T) 280
                Converg <u>− 3</u>
                       277
              Plot   097 direct from the station
    The convergence being 4 x 0·8 = 3°
              Fix <u>5338N 0209E</u>   (b)
    Distance run on TMG in 35 min = 128 nm = G/S 219 kt
              W/V <u>320/34</u> (Tr and G/S)   (c)

Southern hemisphere
The application of convergence in the Southern hemisphere follows the rules again;
it is added if the bearing True is more than 180, subtracted if less.

    While you are fairly conversant with this topic and its complexities, it may be
opportune to have a look at the chapter in volume 3 'Navigation General'.

4: Sundry Comments on Navigational Plotting

Most of the methods of obtaining fixes have been mentioned as far as the plotting of them is concerned: straight pinpoints, Loran or Gee fixes are only slung into an examination plot mainly to get all the plotters to the same place for ease of marking: the activity is centred normally round position lines, demanding a Track and G/S, if only DR, for their transference. And the P/Ls are usually radio, as they are in flight, and thus G/Cs: we've done the routine methods of plotting them, converting them to R/Ls if using a Mercator, nothing is plotted that is not True (confusing QDR, QDM, forgetting to apply variation at the station are common errors brought on entirely by examination twitch) and so on. A Fix from DME and QDM shows up occasionally, very easy, as it is meant to be: and don't forget an RMI reading is just a QDM.

Another type of P/L is the Consol Bearing, the theoretical breakdown of which is in volume 1 'Radio Aids'. This is an aural radio aid, long range (a good 1 000 miles day or night). The listener counts a series of dots/dashes from a starting signal which includes the call sign: the dots/dashes or dashes/dots merge during each burst into a equisignal and the signals must add up to 60 before the next burst begins: one could finish a count with say, 41 dots 15 dashes, which means 4 signals have been lost in the equisignal: the reading is meaned to give 43 dots, 17 dashes, and this count would be referred to as 43 dots for plotting purposes. A dozen or less G/C bearings are available for such a count from the station tuned in, and the appropriate one must be chosen. These bearings are often printed on charts as ·20, ·30, ·40 and so on, and the interpolated P/L readily plotted, as the appropriate sector is quickly discernible near to DR Track. The more primitive extraction of the P/L is done from CAP 59, and this is used in the exam. As a sample, 43 dots on STAVANGER gives True bearings from it of 011·9, 038·8, 059·8, 079·9, and so on (love those decimals of a degree). The DR position at the time of taking the count must be known more or less to select the appropriate bearing. They are G/Cs, and can be plotted direct on a chart where the G/C is a straight line; if using a Mercator, Appendix III gives, for each station, the conversion angle per change longitude and instructions on how to apply it as if you didn't know: interpolation is simple, or, if change longitude 5° for example, read off for 50 and divide by 10.

The Charts generally used in the ATPL Exam are Mercator, scale 1: 3 000 000 at some quoted latitude: they are biggish sheets, clear to work on, with some facilities and coastlines shown: precision in plotting is called for, though, so keep your pencil sharpened. For practice exercises, from ATPL papers previously set (both ATPL and CPL are obtainable from CAA Pubs., 37 Gratton Road, Cheltenham), and charts from British Airways, Ruislip, Middlesex. The chart sheet is always given at the beginning of the plot question paper.

A Handy Reference Check for Plotting
Nothing is ever plotted that is not True.
Every line must have its proper arrows.
A symbol must have a time.
Heading and TAS

      Refer to Air

      i.e.

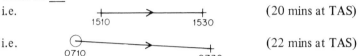

            1510   1530   (20 mins at TAS)

      i.e.   (22 mins at TAS)

            0710   0732

Track and G/S
      Refer to Ground

      i.e.

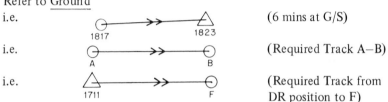

            1817   1823   (6 mins at G/S)

      i.e.   (Required Track A–B)

            A   B

      i.e.   (Required Track from

            1711   F   DR position to F)

Wind Velocity
      Wind speed from a definite direction.
      Wind blows from air position to Fix or to DR position.
      Wind effect is wind for the time since the last Fix.
      i.e. wind effect for 29 mins:

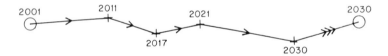

      i.e. using wind effect for 30 mins:

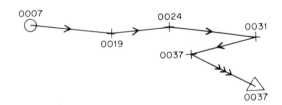

Fix
      Where you know you are.
DR Position
      Where you hope you are.
      It can only be on a Track, never on a Heading.
Air Plot
      A plot of Headings flown, the time of each at TAS.
      It can only be started from a Fix.
      It must be re-started from a Fix.
      It can be carried on from an Air Position.

And it can be carried on for ever, knowing Heading & TAS.

Conversion Angle

Converts a Great Circle to a Rhumb Line, or vice-versa.

All radio bearings are Great Circles.

On Mercator, all straight lines are Rhumb Lines.

$CA = \frac{1}{2}$ ch Long x sin mean Lat or use the ABAC scale.

1. Relative bearing measured in the aircraft + Hdg(T) ± CA then plot reciprocal from the station.

2. QDM, QDR, QTE.

   Get to True.

   Deduce bearing from the station.

   Apply CA then plot from the station.

Convergence

Allows for the convergence of the meridians on Lamberts where G/Cs are straight lines; must be considered when the a/c's Hdg is part of a plotting calculation.

Convergence = Ch long x n

or

Transfer the a/c's meridian to the station if measurement has taken place at that meridian.

If a station gives a bearing, plot what he measured True direct from the station. No question of convergency arises as you are plotting what he measured from his meridian.

5: Grid Navigation

Here we will touch only on the practical plotting on a Grid chart, as the theory of the system is discussed fully in the companion volume 3 'Navigation General'. The use of the Grid chart for air navigation is the easiest thing in the world, overprinted on any chart with converging meridians.

A reference meridian is paralleled across the chart in an outstanding colour, and this Grid Line is used to measure angles, ignoring the meridians, to obtain, for example, a Track (G). Also dotted across the chart are the Grid Variation isogonals, called lines of Grivation. Before you mutter any imprecations, the happy word is that:

Track (G) ± Grivation = Track (M) and the sign of Grivation is treated as for Variation. Similarly for a Heading, of course, so that you at once have the Heading (M) to steer, and all problems of angular measurement on a chart with converging meridians are avoided.

A Heading (G) will in fact differ from the Heading (T) at any meridian by the convergence between that meridian and the reference meridian. This convergence has been applied algebraically to the Variation to give Grivation so that:

Heading (G) ± Grivation = Heading (T) ± Variation.

When working on the Chart, then, all angles (including W/V) can be used quite satisfactorily in Grid.

Have a check on the following run down, on a bit of the gridded Lambert Chart, N. Atlantic (see Fig. 5.1): the reference meridian on this one is in fact the Greenwich meridian, and n for the sheet is given as 0·748819, another way of saying 0·75. Convergence thus becomes for the N. Atlantic Lambert:

ch long x 0·75

A 5000N 4000W to B 5500N 5000W

   (i)   Measured from the 45W meridian: Mean G/C Track 310
                                          R/L Track 310

         Convergence = ch long x n
                    = 10 x 0·75
                    = 8°

        This gives the initial G/C Track of 314 (R/L 310 + $\frac{1}{2}$ Convergence)
              and final G/C Track of 306 (R/L 310 $-\frac{1}{2}$ Convergence)

  (ii) Now the mean G/C Track of 310, keeping to the 45W meridian, would be 340 (M).
        The Grid Track there is 344 (G)
           Grivation there is 4E
        giving a Track of 340 (M), no different from the basic solution. The Grid can be used overall, holding the a/c on the mean G/C, avoiding the com-

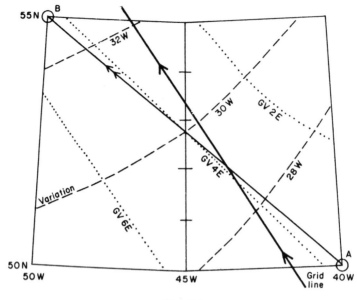

Fig. 5.1

plications of the converging meridians.

There must be no mixing, of course; all the information in Grid will evolve the correct navigational information. Take this example, on the computer:

Conventionally: Mean G/C Track 310 (T), TAS 300 kt
                  W/V 250/40
                  ∴ Hdg 303(T), Var 30W
                  = Hdg 333(M) and G/S 280 kt

Grid: Track 344(G), TAS 300 kt
                  W/V 284/40(G)
                  ∴ Hdg 337(G), Griv 4E
                  = Hdg 333(M) and G/S 280 kt

The relationship between Track(T) and Track(G) is the value of the convergence of the reference meridian or Grid line and the longitude in question; in this case, just a straight 45 x 0·75 = 34°, as the Grid line is the Greenwich meridian.

6: Radio Navigation Charts

These are commonly called Aerad Charts and are published by the International Aeradio Ltd. They are reprinted the moment any alteration is made to a factual detail, so any chart you have before you while going through this chapter is hardly likely to agree in every point with the one we are quoting from. They are available for nearly all areas of the world where navigation can be carried out by the use of radio, whether from the ground or from within the aircraft, with no real plotting required. Skilful use of all radio aids plus adept handling of the computer are sufficient for position finding and accurate ETAs: additionally, complete reporting to the appropriate authority is essential so that the aircraft's position and height are known at any moment in flight. A definite route between reporting points must be followed. It is usual on a trip of this nature to prepare two Flight Plans, one the Fuel Flight Plan such as we shall shortly be much exercised with, using Mean Tracks; the other the Airways Flight Plan, detailing each leg with Tracks (M), Hdgs(M), distances and times, together with details of communications frequencies, and of frequencies of the aids to be used.

Nowadays, every aircraft in flight is under strict ground control and reports must be made at specified points on Track: an ocean crossing cannot be made on Airways, though Track must be adhered to within tight laid-down limits and neither height nor Track can be amended in flight without the Controller's permission. An airway may be laid-down over the desert with not quite the same tightness of control, but the distances between reporting points are often great (and the range of the radio aids often leaves much to be desired too), so that pure navigation is called for. Over most land areas, however, the main trouble is the multiplicity of radio aids, and only experience will teach the pilot which to use, ignore or doubt. The Airways coverage means less and less navigation, but plenty of hard work in the cockpit: a guarantee of safety if the rules are obeyed exactly, the radio aids used skilfully, and the Controller's instructions carried out ably. Rules of communications are established prohibiting chatter of an idle nature — there's no time anyway.

The charts are now all in Lambert's projection and are printed in grey, black and blue.

Europe 1 and 2
The following information is to be found in black:

Airway centrelines	Graticule figures
Radio facilities	Bearings and radials
Control zone boundaries	CTR, TMA, ATZ limits
FIR and ASR boundaries	Aerodromes and names, when with radio facilities

Under the blue colour look for variation (isogonal) lines at the top and bottom edges of the chart, danger, restricted and prohibited areas, aerodromes and names if off the Airways or if without radio facilities, training and military areas, coastlines and lakes, quite pretty really.

TMA and sub-TMA boundaries are in grey.

Now to learn to recognise things on the chart:

Controlled Airspace

Airspace left uncoloured on the chart (and this applies to other specification charts) — that is, all airspace shown in white — is controlled airspace. The rules regarding a flight in controlled airspace are fully dealt with in our companion volume *Aviation Law for Pilots.*

Airway

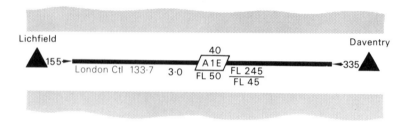

Fig. 6.1

1. Airway centre line is shown in thick black line, with the name of the airway in the centre. In Fig. 6.1 it is Amber 1E.
2. Immediately on top of the Airway name is the distance figure. This is the distance between two reporting points, compulsory or on request, the triangles at start and finish in Fig. 6.1. In this case the distance is 40 nm (all distances are in nautical miles) between Daventry and Lichfield and both these are compulsory reporting points. But even if one was an on-request reporting point, the distance would read the same.

   Be careful when extracting distances. Distance breakdown occurs between reporting points and can happen between a reporting point and a sector point (X) on the route. If you have time, open up your dividers between two points and check the figure against the nautical mile scale (and not, please not, against kilometre) given on top of the chart. If after a rough check your distance agrees reasonably with the printed distance, take printed distance. If you have made a careful check and the printed distance agrees within 2—3 miles, take the printed distance.

   However, the printers do make mistakes and if your measured distance disagrees with the printed distance beyond above limits, take the measured distance, but do point out in your answers in an examination why you are using measured distance.
3. Tracks

   Track angles are given at the beginning, immediately after the facility/reporting point. These tracks are Magnetic. In fact, no tracks, headings, bearings or radials

on this (or any other Aerad) chart are True — they are all Magnetic. A one-way
airway would have the track shown on one end only: the airway designation box
indicates that the airway is one way, thus:

4.   Minimum Flight Level
     The minimum flight level available on that particular sector of the airway is given
     immediately below the Airway designation: FL 50 in Fig. 6.1. This is the lowest
     level you can apply and get clearance for flight on this sector.
        In mountainous territory it would be too risky to give a minimum flight level.
     Here, it will be given in terms of altitude, e.g. 14 000. Examples occur in the
     Zurich area, and the pilot merely flies odd or even thousands of feet on QNH,
     i.e. with the regional barometric setting given by Control; this will read altitude
     above mean sea level. (The full story is given in the altimeter chapter in volume 3.)
     Alternatively, the minimum flight limit may be defined in terms of both, FL and
     altitude, e.g.

                             FL 50
                       (Min. Alt. 4 500)

     This simply means that FL 50 is available for flight provided it at least equates
     4 500 feet on QNH.

5.   Airway Vertical Limits
     Airway vertical limits must not be confused with minimum flight levels. These
     vertical limits legally define the controlled airspace forming an airway, CTR,
     TMA, etc. In our illustration the airway out from Daventry stretches from FL 45
     (the base of the Airway) to FL 245 (the ceiling of the Airway—Upper Airways
     starts at FL 250 anyway). If these limits were to change, a pecked line at right
     angles to the airway centre line would indicate where the change takes place, and
     the ceiling and base limits would be printed on each side of this dividing line.
     This lowering of the base does not affect the minimum flight level available for
     flight on the sector.
        The easiest way to distinguish between the two is: where FL or Altitude figure
     stands on its own on the chart it is the lowest limit at which the flight can be made;
     where FL or Alt appear in the form of a fraction, then those are the vertical limits
     imposed.
        It may be mentioned that the base of an airway, or TMA need not be in terms
     of FL, it may be given as altitude as well, e.g. the vertical limits of Amber 2
     between Brookmans Park and Detling are

                             FL 245
                             ───────
                             3 500

     Does it make any difference? Fly QNH, 3 500 ft on the clock, and you are on the
     airway base.
        Lastly, in the U.K. there is at least a 500 ft clearance between the base of the
     airway and the lowest aircraft on the airway.

6. Terrain Clearance
    A figure 3·0 for example, below the centre line and to the left of the airway
    designation box indicates, in thousands (thus 3 000), the altitude of the highest
    ground within 30 nm of the airway centre line to either side, and a semi-circle,
    radius 30 nm at either end of the sector giving this value.

That's just about all as far as airway symbols are concerned. We must warn you that
the layout shown above (Fig. 6.1) is the ideal layout. In congested areas, information
may be scattered all over the place. Now for the remaining symbols that you will see
on the chart.

Reporting Points
Small triangles, as shown above at Daventry and Lichfield. A full black triangle (complete block) is a compulsory reporting point and you must report there. A hollow
black triangle is an 'On Request' reporting point.

Facilities

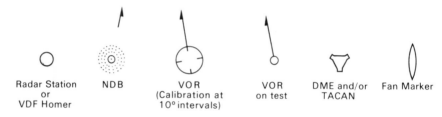

| Radar Station or VDF Homer | NDB | VOR (Calibration at 10° intervals) | VOR on test | DME and/or TACAN | Fan Marker |

Fig. 6.2

NDBs. Those tiny black flags above NDB symbols (but some distance away) are not
indicative of holes at the local golf course. The flag direction is the direction of Magnetic North at the NDB below it. The flag to the west of the vertical line indicates
westerly variation. In Fig. 6.2, the variation is easterly.

VORs. The direction of Magnetic North is indicated by a line with a flag at its top,
from the 000° radial. The convention regarding easterly/westerly variation applies.
    Note that a VOR on test has a special symbol (circle without calibration points)
whereas an NDB on test has no separate symbol. In practice, an NDB is not inserted
on the chart until it becomes fully operational.

TACAN/DME. Although ICAO has separated the two, a single symbol is used on
Aerads to indicate both. The separation is achieved in the information box, see below.

Fan Marker. A few of them are still left on airways in the U.K., plentiful everywhere
in connection with ILS. You require a 75 MHz receiver to get the signals.

Facility Frequencies
Against each facility symbol, the call sign and frequencies of the radio facilities are
given. CAM 332·5 for example is CAMBRIDGE NDB on frequency 332·5 kHz, call

sign CAM. In no time flat after some experience you will recognise VORs, NDBs, TACANs and so on, just from the frequencies given. On actual Airways, the information is enclosed in a box. CAM has no official route going through it.

Another point to note is that the Cambridge NDB frequency CAM 332·5 is not in quotes whereas Birmingham NDB 'GX' 347 is in quotes. What is the difference between the two? Well, the one not in quotes has A1 emission; the one in quotes has A2 emission. The full story about A1 and A2 emissions is given in volume 1 'Radio Aids'.

Fan markers operate on the single frequency of 75 MHz, and therefore this frequency is not repeated on the charts. At a Fan marker, you will see:

Compton
· · — —

that is, name, and call sign in Morse. It is at the bottom of EUR 1, at 0100W, and that's a frequency recently changed.

As for DME and TACAN let us take a look at the following frequencies noted on the chart.

Coningsby	Wallasey	Barton
CGY Ch 48	WAZ Ch 88	BTN 112·4
(111·1)	WAL 114·1	Ch 7 (DME)

Coningsby facility is VORTAC. VOR transmits on 111·1 MHz and if you are carrying a DME receiver, aerial and indicator, the indicator will be activated automatically giving ranges from Coningsby. The callsign will be merged with VOR callsign CGY.

The Wallasey facility is a TACAN. If you have a DME channel selector, select Ch 88; otherwise, with DME equipment on board, select 114·1 on VOR. In either case you will receive ranges from Wallasey, and the callsign will be WAZ. The letter Z indicates that the facility may be used in conjunction with the neighbouring VOR whose frequency is equivalent to Ch 88 (i.e. 114·1). Z also indicates that the two facilities are not co-located or associated ('associated' is used here as it is legally defined; see the chapter on DME in volume 1).

Barton has pure DME, frequency paired with Barton VOR frequency 112·4. This is now pretty general on the busy U.K./EUR. routes.

Control Zones, Special Rules Zones/Areas, Military ATZs
These are officially abbreviated CTRs, SRZ/SRAs, (Mil) ATZs on the chart and are shown as uncoloured (white) areas enclosed by black pecked lines. The vertical limits are given as a fraction, immediately below the name of the zone:

Scampton	East Midlands	Honiton
(Mil) ATZ	SRZ	(Mil) CTR
3 460		4 000
g		g

Honiton is also signified as a Danger area, as activity there is intense. If a military area is away from the civil routes, and the vertical limits are low, then it is shown on a grey background.

Altimeter Setting Regions (ASRs)

These are shown by longish pecked lines in black, the lines defining the boundaries. The names of the regions appear somewhere along the pecked lines, and when you cross this line, you should change your altimeter setting to the QNH value of the region you are entering.

FIR Boundaries

Fig. 6.3

The name of the FIR, its ICAO four-letter code, and the upper limit of the FIR which in each case is FL 245 is given. It is worth mentioning that the FIR does not have to be a straight line: try the boundary from about 5100N 0600E on EUR 1 for Dusseldorf and Amsterdam (and Amsterdam FIR isn't even printed on the boundary — it is on the Lon/Amst boundary at about 2 o'clock from 5120N 0200E, and it is split into West and East sectors, noted around 5230N 0330E, for example).

Bearings and Radials

These generally define reporting points, where they are not co-located with radio facilities; in the main they are on-request points. There are a few left, but now they are invariably radials, as illustrated in Fig. 6.4. If you do come across an odd NDB bearing, follow the line down to the NDB itself where the bearing figure is inserted.

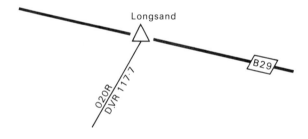

Fig. 6.4

In Fig. 6.4 reporting point Longsand on B29 is defined by a VOR radial. The presentation is standard on all Aerad charts: 020°R simply means it is on 020° radial from VOR that is traced at the other end of the bearing line. In this particular case since Dover VOR is not on this side of the chart, its reference is added here in terms of its callsign and frequency.

Advisory Routes (ADRs)

Designation of all advisory routes up to FL 245 is by the letter D as first letter, e.g. DRI (Lower ADR Red One). These will be recognised on the chart by grey areas (grey because ADRs are uncontrolled) delimited by white outlines on either side of the centre line. The practical aspect of flight on ADRs is fully investigated in *Aviation Law for Pilots*.

You will find, out of Ottringham, for example, a series of routes over the North Sea simply designated:

These are approved routes over uncongested areas, and the little tab in the corner is to tell you that the distances have been calculated by Aeradio themselves, and they are therefore unofficial as it were, but they like to be helpful.

All airways and ADRs are 10 nm wide (5 nm either side of the centre line) in this country.

In blue you will see the outlines of restricted airspace (Danger, Restricted and Prohibited areas), TMA boundaries, isogonals and graticule outlines.

Danger Areas

Danger Areas should be checked before flight; the chart shows permanent Danger/ Restricted areas as a continuous blue line; temporary ones (that is, those activated by Notam) are shown by small pecked lines. Prohibited areas are filled in with tiny dots.

On the last fold on each side of the chart you will find the Airspace Restriction Panel which sorts out Danger and Restricted areas (which otherwise look alike on the chart: continuous line if permanent or during published hours, broken if temporary) and give pertinent details about those and prohibited areas. It is necessary that you are able to decode printers' shorthand. Here are a few examples, taken from 'France'.

R1 820–2 600 g HN M–F

R1 is the ident of the Area, and the area concerned is a restricted area (R). Limits 820–2 600 g imply the figures are on QNH (above the ground), and it is restricted to Night hours M–F only. Quite a biggie, this one, if you trace it round.

R2 FL 55 Permanent

Here the limit is from ground or sea whichever happens to occupy the area up to FL 55 (on 1 013·2 setting).

D43 FL 30–55 HJ VMC M–F and Notified

This is a Danger Area (D), limits are obvious but under the remarks column we have been given times of operation: daylight hours if VMC M–F or when notified in Notam.

If the limit was given, say, as 1 000–FL 55, it means both limits on 1 013·2. 1 000 above ground is given as 1 000 g. Other abbreviations used are:

Unltd – unlimited.

Wkd – weekdays, Monday to Saturday (inc.).

M is Monday, Tu is Tuesday, and so on.

HJ daylight hours (proof of the mapmakers' deep knowledge of the French tongue).

HN – night.

agl – above ground level.

TMA Boundaries

These are perhaps the most difficult ones to spot. Main boundary and all sub-divisions of the TMA within it are shown by white areas (controlled airspace) bounded by thickish grey lines. What makes it difficult to trace is the fact that these boundaries generally run along the outer boundaries of Airways — just where the white colour finishes and the grey starts — and the lines seem to merge with the background grey. However, with a little practice you will soon be able to keep it in sight. Try Scottish TMA for a starter.

Isogonals
These are shown as blue pecked lines, lightly started and ended only, at top and bottom of the chart. The date and annual change is noted in the legend box inserted somewhere on the chart.

Miscellaneous
1. Authorised routes (which are neither airways nor ADRs) are shown by black thin lines, with track and arrow at both ends if the route is two-way; if it is one-way, the route line ends with an arrow.
2. Quite a few States publish Flight Plan codes for reporting points. Where these are available, the pertinent letters in the name of the reporting point are underlined, thus: Matching.
3. When a reporting point is abeam a facility, and this is a part of its definition, it is shown thus:

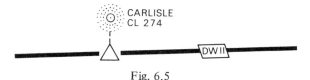

CARLISLE
CL 274

Fig. 6.5

The name of this reporting point is 'Abeam' Carlisle Beacon, and don't forget if you have got 8° starboard drift when you are nicely on Track lined up with departure or destination radials, then you're abeam CARLISLE on a relative bearing of 278.

4. Airway Frequencies
In the U.K. you will find appropriate airway frequencies noted along the airway. The symbol denoting a communication sector boundary is:

    ..   ..

On Europe 2 you will notice that the frequencies are not given along the airways. Most of the countries on the continent sectorise the territory into convenient communication sectors, and the frequency for use in a particular sector is given in a prominent (so they say) place inside the sector (usually boxed).

Paris Ctl   Brussels Awys
TN Sector   West Sector
131·35   131·1
Paris Control and Brussels Airways are the callsigns.
More frequencies are listed on the front fold of the chart — CTR, FIS, Met and so forth. Have a look at them.

5. Flight Levels
Semi-circular rules apply on airways, and Aerad invariably inserts 'odd' and

'even' as appropriate on the airways. These are sometimes left out in cluttered areas. In the absence of these, fly odd thousands when Tr(M) lies between 000–179; fly evens when Tr(M) between 180–359. This is, however, only a general rule and many exceptions occur (perhaps you remember that rules of quadrantal and semi-circular flying do not apply in controlled airspace in IFR: you fly the level given you).

6. Coastal NDBs
Some of these NDBs do not provide continuous service.

Cromer

'CM' 287·3

H + 04 & Ev. 6 mins

This NDB only transmits short bursts of CM in morse for 1 minute at 4 minutes past the hour and repeats every 6 minutes thereafter.

Information not on Europe 1/2
Any information on routes and airways at FL 250 and above is contained in High Level chart H108/109.

Information on holding (holding point, pattern, time and min. alt.) is contained in a panel on 'area charts'.

The remaining symbols on Eur 1/2 are

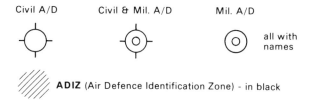

Notes on Airway Flying
1. To stress the point again, distances are given between compulsory or on-request reporting points, the solid or open black triangles, most of the time, also between intersection or turning points marked with a cross, so watch it.
2. A report is no longer required on crossing a boundary from one Information Region to another, but you must be aware you have crossed it for your subsequent reports. The parallel of latitude 55N from 0500E to 0530W is marked with a pecked line indicating such a boundary, and the name of the appropriate FIR region set on either side of it, London & Scottish. Three boundaries meet on the 0530W meridian at 5355N, for example, easy to recognise here, but on B29 on 294M out of Nicky near Brussels the boundary is a winding river which is crossed 4 times in about 30 nm.
3. A report is made only to the Air Traffic Control Centre (ATCC) of the Flight Information Region (FIR) in which the aircraft is flying: thus, a report in the London FIR is to London Airways.
4. The message content is crisp and its form invariable, once communication has been established (Scottish Airways, this is Golf Alpha Sierra Tango on 124·9, do you read?). 'Scottish Airways, this is Golf Alpha Sierra Tango, Lichfield 27,

Flight Level 80, estimate Oldham 39, over'. That's all. Who you are, where you are, your Flight Level, ETA next point, over, and memorise the form.

Let us take a trip from BROOKMANS PARK (5145N 0006W) to PRESTWICK (5529N 0436W) via Amber 2 and Amber 1 part of which is shown on page 51 (from EUR 1).

BROOKMANS PARK is a compulsory reporting point with an NDB callsign (c/s) BPK, frequency 328 kHz. The c/s is in quotes so it is A2 emission, tune on CW, identify on RT. This station is in fact a de-control point from London Airport. FL is 'even', so suggest FL 80: instructions in conjunction with the filed Flight plan would be given by London Airways.

WOBURN is next reporting point, on request only, distance 29 nm, Tr 312 (M).

DAVENTRY is a compulsory reporting point, track unaltered, distance 17 nm. VOR facility c/s DTY, freq. 116·4 MHz. DME is available on Channel 111, and this will give a distance presentation in suitably-equipped aircraft simply by tuning in the VOR frequency or DME channel.

All reports of the a/c's position are passed to London Control on 135·25 as noted at DAVENTRY.

From DAVENTRY to LICHFIELD on A1E, the track is 335M, distance 40 nm. Check any change in FL: the bottom of the Airway changes but our FL 80 is still all right. Reports to London Control now on 133·7.

LICHFIELD has NDB, c/s LIC, frequency 545 kHz, 355M to Polehill. Whether to report to Lon Ctl on 131·05 or Manchester Ctl on 126·65 depends on Flight Level – above FL 130 to Lon, below to Manchester: at FL 80, we report to Manchester. The distance of 20 nm takes us to a pecked line across Track: up to then, the bottom of the Airway is FL 55, provided this gives a QNH altitude of 4 500 ft: after it, the base is FL 45, QNH 3 500 at least.

OLDHAM, on request, NDB c/s OLD, frequency 344, and in quotes so A2, tune on CW, identify on RT. Notice LIC – divider is 20 nm, then to OLD 30, OLD–POL 11, and the last distance is not entered on the chart: minimum FL is 60, and terrain clearance 3 600 ft amsl for 30 nm range from the centre line and OLDHAM itself.

To POLEHILL VOR, c/s POL, frequency 112·1, Track 355M but terrain clearance now 3 800 ft. Our FL 80 still okay.

To DEAN CROSS, and we are on the pukka A1 now, a compulsory reporting point, VOR, c/s DCS, frequency 115·2, DME available (as at Daventry) on channel 99, Track 332M, 73 nm. There are three dividers splitting the route, altering the lower limit of the Airway on four sections: the first is 3500 on QNH, the second 4500 on QNH, the third is FL 55, the fourth is FL 65, but this last must also be at least 5500 on QNH. Our FL 80 is okay, and Lon Ctl still not available at our FL, report to Manchester on 133·05. The last divider cuts an on-request reporting point BLN, which has no aids whatever, and it is 20 nm from Polehill; if a report is wanted there, rely on VOR radial and DME from POL.

On the way to Prestwick (PIK), Track 315, 39 nm, to AGY, an on-request reporting point which is abeam New Galloway NGY 399, with lower limit changing from FL 65 (QNH 5500) to 4000 on QNH we shall cross the FIR boundary 29 nm from DCS, and a report is advisable to London Ctl on 132·7, and Scottish A/ways on 128·5 or 124·9, depending on the time of day.

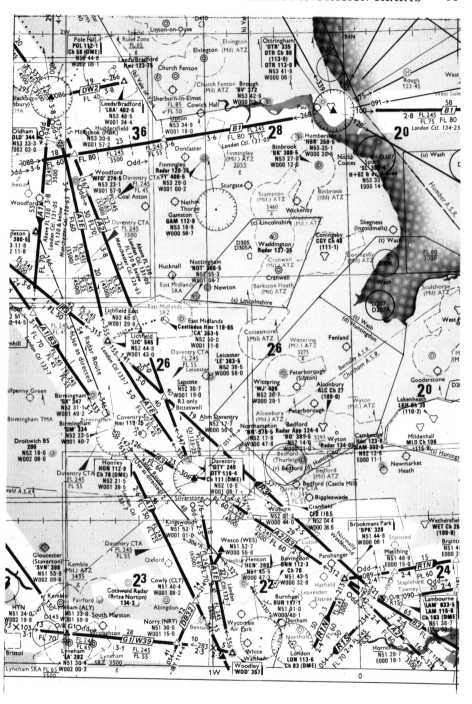

PRESTWICK has VOR c/s PWK, frequency 117·5, DME on Channel 122. Unless instructed, FL would be maintained, but near AGY we enter a large area shown in white and labelled 'Scottish TMA'. As a landing is intended, communication with the TMA is made as soon as permissible; the frequency is given on the margin fold. Instructions will now flow in. The Transition Altitude (TA) is given, and so on, until you are finally ordered to contact PIK for landing instructions.

A larger scale Area Chart is available for busy areas shown on these charts by black double-lined rectangles: Scottish TMA, Belfast Routes, Manchester Area, Birmingham Routes are examples. Also, each airfield has its Approach charts. Area charts are simply blown up charts of the areas shown on the Aerads in a 'picture frame'. Further information is given to ease the pilot's load when in a busy area, calling for prompt attention to Control instructions. There is no change in symbols, etc., but holding points and patterns, communication frequencies for the various airports when departing therefrom or arriving thereto, special charts for specific aerodromes with their departure/arrival routes are clearly shown.

Approach charts simply blow up the facilities at a particular aerodrome, and give every detail about them.

High Altitude charts, labelled with an H, such as H108/109, are similar to the types we have been studying. They are for flight at or above FL 250, and since greater speeds are involved, the interval between reporting points is greater; reports are made to Upper Air Information Regions (UIRs) mainly coincident with FIRs.

Tracks, distances, bearings, frequencies: all these change from time to time, changes incorporated every 28 days by Airac Notams. So, if any of the above information does not match your chart, do not worry, so long as you understand what we are trying to convey.

Before leaving the topic, it is convenient to run over Transition Altitude, Transition Level and Transition Layer. The Spaniards have their own solution which is tabulated on the chart, but the accepted way is mainly held to internationally. On take-off and landing, climb and descent, they are quite distinct.

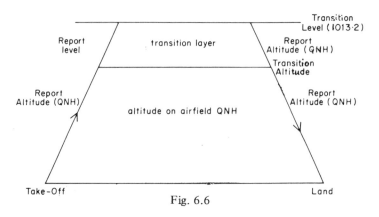

Fig. 6.6

The airfield QNH is given. Transition Altitude is always specified; it must be at least 1 500 ft above the aerodrome, and it is usually 4 000 ft in Controlled Airspace,

3 000 ft outside. The Transition Level is the lowest FL available for use above the Transition Altitude. The depth of the Transition Layer can cause some confusion; the idea is to make this as thin as possible. Take an airfield QNH of 1 003 mb, Transition Altitude 4 000 ft, Transition Level 50; the moment the Transition Altitude is passed on the climb, the altimeter is set to 1 013 mb which will make it register 4 300 ft; thus, the Transition Layer is 700 ft thick. The Transition Level merely refers to a FL in any direction, and there is no involvement with the FL the a/c is finally going to settle at. A QNH of 1 013 mb could give the ideal, no Transition Layer at all, while a QNH higher than 1 013 mb would deepen the Transition Layer.

The Aerad charts are of course constantly being brought up to date, and the operational use of the very latest issue is imperative.

Now try this exercise, using an available EUR 2 for the latter part.
You are planning a flight from STUTTGART (4842N 0913E) to REIMS (4919N 0403E) via G5, R7 and R10. You join the airway G5 at TANGO reporting point, and leave at MONTMEDY VOR. TAS 200. You are equipped with twin ADR, VOR and DME. Descent from MONTMEDY VOR.

1.   In absence of any other information, are you expected to fly ODD flight levels or EVEN flight levels?
2.   Give a complete list of all points where you must make position reports. Have you any option anywhere?
3.   State TANGO NDB frequency, ident and type of emission.
4.   Is there any facility at TANGO from which you could receive range 'out' information? If so, state how you would use it.
5.   About half way between TANGO and ROTTWEIL a thin line cuts your track at an angle. The line ends with figures 123°R. What purpose does this line serve?
6.   Arriving at ROTTWEIL reporting point, who would you pass your position report to, and where is the frequency to be found?
7.   Between ROTTWEIL and STRASBOURG:
   (a)   what is your track?
   (b)   what is the distance?
   (c)   below airway centre line, this information is given:

$$6{\cdot}8\,\frac{FL\,160}{FL\,90}$$

give the meaning of each item.

Nearing STRASBOURG you cross a broken, curving line in black which is superimposed on a continuous blue line.

8.   What is this black line for, and why it is broken?
9.   What is the purpose of the blue line beneath?
10.   Just before crossing this line, in whose TMA are you flying?
11.   Are you also flying in any CTR at this time?
12.   How would you know when you are overhead STRASBOURG?

You leave STRASBOURG VOR at 1000 hrs on heading 322°(M) for GROS TENQUIN. Your VOR is tuned to STR frequency with 316° on OBS, your Radio compass is also tuned to STR. TAS say 280 kt.

13.   Assuming you remain on track, what readings do you expect on the VOR and Radio compass?

You arrive overhead GROS TENQUIN at 1011 hrs —

14.   What W/V was experienced on this leg?
15.   What is your ETA at next reporting point?
16.   How would your navigation equipment be tuned on this leg?

17.   You are cleared to overhead LUXEMBOURG VOR, and arrive at 1022, FL 180. Give your full position report and state to whom you will pass your report and on what frequency. (Assume the W/V remains unchanged.)
18.   What information would you expect to receive in return?
19.   When at MONTMEDY VOR who would you pass your position report to, and request permission to leave airway and proceed to REIMS? On what frequency?
20.   Are you now in PARIS TMA?
21.   On your last leg to REIMS while descending you decide to hear the Met report from PARIS. What frequency will you tune to for this?
22.   What navigation facilities are available at REIMS which you could use?
23.   Between GROS TENQUIN and LUXEMBOURG the airway is covered by some kind of restricted airspace. What can you tell about it?
24.   Why is Germany shown with a white background whereas France, Belgium and Luxembourg have areas of grey?
25.   Were you ever in BRUSSELS FIR? If so, where did you enter, and leave?

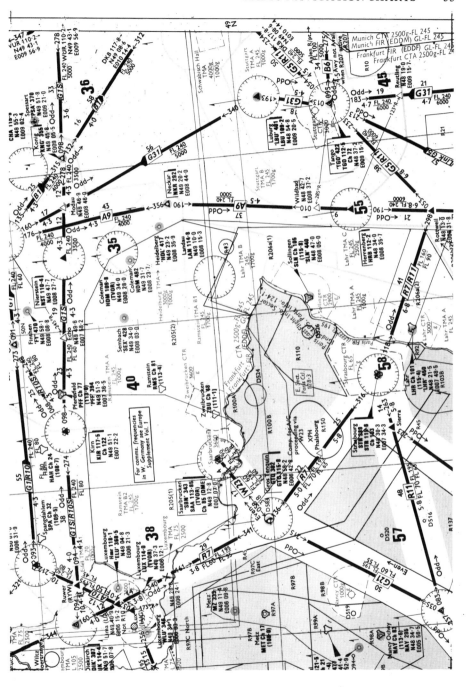

7: Relative Motion

Relative Speed

Whenever two aircraft are in motion, each aircraft has a speed which is relative to the other. Two aircraft flying in formation at a given speed, have a relative speed with regard to each other: it is zero speed, because neither aircraft is going ahead or falling behind. If two aircraft are approaching on reciprocal tracks, aircraft A doing a speed of 150 kt and aircraft B speed of 200 kt, then each aircraft has a speed of 350 kt relative to the other. We call this the closing speed. Again, if an aircraft A with ground speed of 350 kt is overtaking aircraft B having a ground speed of 300 kt, each aircraft's relative speed is 50 kt, whereas aircraft A's closing speed is 50 kt. Therefore, if the two aircraft were initially separated by, say, 100 nm aircraft A will be alongside B in two hours.

Example. Two aircraft A and B are initially separated by 200 nm and are approaching each other. A's ground speed is 300 kt, B's ground speed is 260 kt. How long will they take to meet?

$$\text{Relative (or closing) speed} = 300 + 260$$
$$= 560 \text{ kt}$$
$$\text{Time taken to meet} = 200 \text{ nm at } 560 \text{ kt}$$
$$= 21\tfrac{1}{2} \text{ min}$$

How far would each have flown before they meet?
Aircraft A with ground speed of 300 kt will travel 107 nm in $21\tfrac{1}{2}$ min
Aircraft B with ground speed of 260 kt will travel 93 nm in $21\tfrac{1}{2}$ min

Practice problems

1. Two planes take off from stations 500 nm apart. They meet in 44 minutes. If the first plane travelled 3/5th of the total distance, find the ground speed of each.
Answer: 410 and 273 kt

2. An aircraft A, flying at ground speed of 390 kt is overtaking aircraft B, flying at ground speed of 310 kt. Two aircraft are initially 50 nm apart.
(a) In how many minutes will aircraft A be 5 nm behind B?
(b) When will aircraft A be 3 minutes behind B?
Answer: (a) $33\tfrac{1}{2}$ minutes; (b) $34\tfrac{1}{2}$ minutes

Relative Direction

When two aircraft are moving, each will have a relative direction with respect to the other. If two aircraft A and B left a point X at the same time, A on a track due North and B on a track due East, then to an observer in aircraft A, B will appear to be tracking SE. To an observer in aircraft B, A will appear to be tracking NW; this is A's relative direction with respect to aircraft B.

Relative Velocity
When a body has velocity, it has both speed and direction, and problems of relative velocity are essentially solved by accurate scale plotting. The first step is to bring to a stop the aircraft which wishes to observe the other.

In above example, say A's ground speed is 400 kt, B's ground speed is 320 kt. To find B's relative velocity with respect to A, bring A to a stop. This is done by imparting A's negative velocity to B. B, therefore, now has two velocities, its own velocity and A's negative velocity. Fig. 7.1.

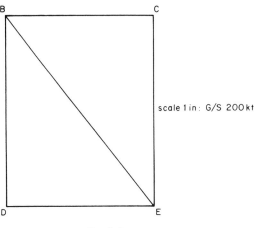

scale 1 in: G/S 200 kt

Fig. 7.1

In Fig. 7.1, BC is B's own velocity, that is, one hour's ground speed due East. BD is A's negative velocity, 400 nm due <u>south</u>. Complete the parallelogram BCED. BE is the relative velocity of B with respect to A which is 140° at 508 kt (by actual measurement).

If A's relative velocity with respect to B is required, B is brought to rest by imparting its negative velocity to A.

Where two flights do not originate at the same point as above, the relative velocity may still be estimated as in following illustration.

Given: Aircraft A's track is 050(T), G/S 210 kt. Aircraft B which bears 140(T) from A is doing a track of 355(T) at G/S250 kt. B is 200 nm from A. Find the relative bearing of B from A.

In these problems since the distance between two aircraft is generally very small in comparison with aircraft speeds, it is necessary to select two different scales, one for ground speed and one for distance in order to separate the two aircraft for neat plotting. In above illustration the ground speed scale chosen is 1 in to 100 kt, and distance scale is 1 in to 50 nm.

Steps
1.   Choose a convenient point A and plot from here A's Track and one hour's ground speed (at ground speed scale) — AC.
2.   From A, plot B on given bearing (140° in above illustration) at a given distance (200 nm) at distance scale — AB.

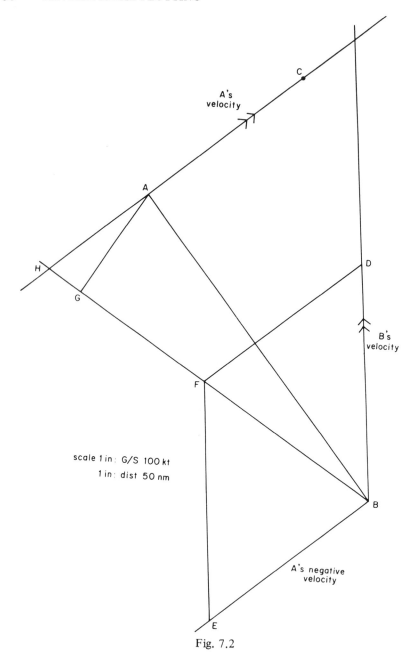

Fig. 7.2

3. From B, plot B's velocity for one hour — BD.
4. From B, draw A's negative velocity for one hour — BE.
5. Complete parallelogram BDFE.
6. Join BF
    BF is B's relative velocity with respect to A — 302° at relative speed of 215 kt.
    The above figure tells us more than just the relative velocity.

Produce BF to intersect A's track at H. If this line intersects A's track exactly through A's position, two aircraft are on such headings and speeds that a collision will occur. If BF produced crosses A's track behind A's position, as in above illustration, B will pass behind A. The shortest distance that A and B will be apart is indicated by AG drawn perpendicular from A to BH, measured at distance scale. Similarly, if BF produced crosses A's track ahead of it, B will pass ahead of A.

The above is true even if distance AB initially is not known.

H is the point where B will cross A's track behind A. AH is the distance – use distance scale.

The time that B will be shortest distance from A is calculated from known information of B's relative ground speed and the distance BG.
In Fig. 7.2, it is 188 nm at 215 kt = $52\frac{1}{2}$ min

Interception
Interceptions are carried out on the principle of maintaining a constant relative bearing. Aircraft A sights another aircraft B on a relative bearing of 140°. If A wishes to intercept B, it must maintain such a heading and TAS that would result in B's relative bearing remaining constant throughout. Fig. 7.3.

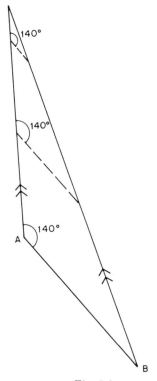

Fig. 7.3

In the above figure, it will be noticed that if the bearing is not maintained constant, aircraft B is either going to fall ahead or behind of A.

In order to carry out an interception, the first step is to establish the positions of both aircraft and plot them. The line joining the two aircraft at any given instant is the bearing that must remain constant. In Fig. 7.4, this is the line AB, and is known as the Line of Constant Bearing.

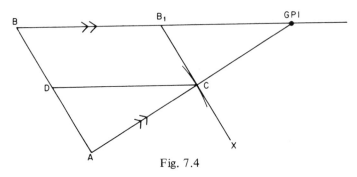

Fig. 7.4

At B, plot B's Track and mark off B_1 to represent one hour's G/S to vector scale. At B_1 draw BX parallel to BA; this is the Line of Constant Bearing.

With centre A and radius A's G/S to scale, inscribe an arc of a circle to cut B_1X at C. Join AC and produce it to meet B's Track at the Ground Position of Interception (GPI).

From C draw CD parallel to B_1B. Then AD to scale represents the speed of closing, while AB is the distance to close at closing speed.

All plotting may be done with Headings and TAS, but it must be borne in mind that the end product is an Air Position of Interception; to find the GPI from this is simply a matter of applying the wind effect for the time taken.

Latest time to divert to an alternate

To find the latest time to divert to an alternate would be worked out on these lines. An aircraft with 5 hours endurance has an alternate to beam of Track. Join departure point A to the alternate B, measure the distance and derive its hypothetical G/S from the endurance. Along both Tracks, using the same vector scale for both, plot the distance covered in one hour; this is the Line of Constant Bearing GF. Produce GF. Still with same vector scale, at A, plot a W/V vector and from it with radius TAS, strike an arc on GF produced at K. Join AK. AK paralleled from B to cut the out-

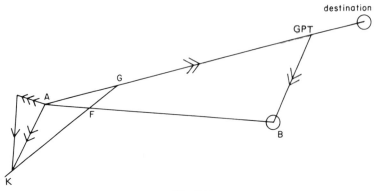

Fig. 7.5

bound Track is the Ground Position of Turning, and the plot contains all the necessary information for the diversion.

Problems

1.   An aircraft A in position 55N 02W is making good a track of 180(T) at ground speed of 210 kt. Aircraft B is flying along parallel of 49°10′N and at 1000 hrs, it bears 220° from A. Both aircraft eventually meet.
     What is B's bearing from A at 1030 hrs?
Answer: 220°(T)

2.   Aircraft A making good a Tr 030(T) at 300 kt passes over B which is making good a track of 310 at 260 kt. Estimate relative velocity of B from A prior to passing over B.
Answer: 255° − 363 kt

3.   Aircraft A on track of 090 is doing ground speed of 200 kt. It will collide with B in 5 min if no alteration to heading is made. B at present is on bearing of 030 relative from A. If B's ground speed is 250 kt, estimate B's track and relative velocity, assuming zero drift.
Answer: Tr 323; Rel.Vel. 300° − 402 kt

4.   Aircraft A whose TAS is 270 observes aircraft B on relative bearing of 040°. Aircraft B observes A on relative bearing of 330°. If two aircraft are on collision headings, determine
(a) TAS of aircraft B;
(b) speed at which the two aircraft are closing.
Answer: (a) 320 kt   (b) 480 kt

5.   An aircraft A is flying due south at ground speed of 170. B is flying East at ground speed of 210 both having left the same point. What is the relative bearing of B with respect to A?
Answer: 050° − 270 kt.

6.   Aircraft A is heading 030(T), TAS 230. Aircraft B which bears 310(T) from A is heading 080(T) at TAS 320 kt. If neither aircraft alters heading or speed, which will pass ahead of the other?
Answer: Aircraft B.

FLIGHT PLANNING

8: Principles of Flight Planning

Introduction

Before flight in the commercial business of carrying passengers or cargo for hire or reward, a very comprehensive Flight Plan must be made, giving the Headings Magnetic to steer, the time on each leg, the fuel to be consumed, the height to fly, the alternates available, and any other detail useful for the trip. It is a plan, a guide, and its main purpose is safety, ensuring primarily that sufficient fuel is uplifted plus a bit extra for mother. In the air, amendments to Headings and times will be made, with a continuous check on fuel consumption and weather ahead, by actual navigation.

The first pre-requisite on arrival at the field is a visit to the Met Office to get a briefing on the forecast weather for the route, and for all the aerodromes likely to be used; forecast Wind Velocities and temperatures at pertinent heights will be given, and from these, the Flight Plan can be filled in. This done, adequate fuel can be ordered and other matters such as range, point of no return can be duly entered. The complete plan will be reported to Air Traffic Control, so that in the air a full surveillance of the aircraft's progress will be kept.

A couple of lines of a Flight Plan might look like the example opposite.

Having gaped at that lot for a moment or two (and perhaps checked the TAS, times, Headings on your computer), you will appreciate that here is most of the information required for the trip and on the trip; but of course, temperatures, Wind Velocities are forecast, fuel consumption may not go according to the book, ETAs will invariably change, but the Plan is there.

You will have remarked that fuel consumption has decreased slightly on the second leg: as the weight of the aircraft decreases with fuel being burned off, so there is less weight to heave through the air, and consumption will be reduced. This is a very broad statement: there's more to it than that, for the power can be reduced to conserve fuel thereby dropping the airspeed, for example; cruise control techniques are various, but experience has cut them down to two basics:

1. **Constant Power**. Keeping the power constant will result in the airspeed increasing as the weight decreases with fuel consumption reasonably constant.

2. **Long Range Cruise**. Power is decreased as the weight reduces to conserve fuel with a TAS reasonably constant.

The refinements of these types are numerous, and airlines and aeroplanes usually have some rule of thumb starters to help the pilot decide in the light of all conditions the safest and most suitable control to select. For quick trips of an internal nature, a short-range cruise control is possible in order to adjust TAS to give a suitable G/S to maintain a tight schedule, with fuel consumption a minor consideration. But generally the two types above are the main ones and a pilot can switch in flight when he likes: with good terminal weather forecast, and ahead of Flight Plan at his en route check

STAGE		Press height ft × 1000	RAS kt	Temp °C	TAS kt	W/V	Tr (T)	Hdg (T)	Var	Hdg (M)	Dist nm	G/S kt	Time min	ETA	Fuel flow kg/hr	Fuel kg
From	To															
ALICE SPRINGS	Abm OODNA	31	258	−45	423	270/60	149	156	5E	151	237	450	32	0447	3900	2080
Abm OODNA	LEIGH	31	258	−46	423	260/60	149	156	6E	150	231	442	31	0518	3860	2000

points, he will reject any further need to conserve fuel, and switch from Long Range Cruise to Constant Power. Or, if terminal weather is forecast poor, with a possibility of a diversion or a long hold in the stack, he will chuck out Constant Power and switch to Long Range Cruise for safety, as the priority is no longer to arrive on time but to be prepared for exigencies.

The Principles of Flight Planning

In the very first place, with the information available before flight, the problem is one of work with the computer to resolve this information into the essentials for the flight itself. After this, as the pilot considers fuel, it is aircraft weight which is the governing factor; this weight decreases dramatically as the trip progresses with the high rate of fuel consumption, and a mean consumption or a mean TAS *per sector* must be deduced. Aircraft manufacturers set out this data in the aircraft manual, and for a 'weight at start' of a leg will, for the altitude and temperature, proffer a consumption for the next hour, or even for only the next half-hour, as we shall see. Such data sheets are used in the ATPL exam, but in CPL the knowledge of principles is introduced, and the averages of consumption or TAS must be calculated.

Let us consider first a Flight Plan for a voyage where the TAS is reasonably constant, or in other words, is given, but the fuel consumption varies as the aircraft's weight reduces.

A snippet from the data:

Consumption (kg/hr) at varying weights (kg)			
70 000	65 000	60 000	55 000
4 200	4 000	3 900	3 800

Take-off wt: 68 500 kg

Climb: Mean TAS 340 kt, time 38 min,
            fuel used 3 900 kg

The body of the flight plan — RAS, G/S, times, distance covered on the climb and descent, ETAs, can be completed straight off. The weight at start is 68 500 kg, so at the top of climb, having used 3 900 kg, it will be 64 600 kg for the commencement of level flight. We need the mean weight on the next leg in order to estimate as closely as possible the average consumption on it. Assume for ease of example that the leg will take one hour; from the table above, after half an hour, about 2 000 kg will have been burnt off, giving a weight in mid-leg of 62 600 kg; using this figure to enter the table, a mean consumption will be extracted of 3 950 kg, rounded off to avoid pedantic digits.

To proceed, the weight at start of the next leg is 60 650 kg (having flown for one hour at a consumption of 3 950 kg/hr from a start of 64 600 kg): say the leg will take 40 min. After 20 min at 3 910 kg/hr — and do not strain here, visual and mental calculation is enough — 1 300 kg will be burnt off and the mean weight may be taken to be 59 350 kg. This weight from the tables gives a consumption of 3 890 kg/hr, which is entered on the plan, and in 40 min will use 2 590 kg, giving a weight at start of the next sector of 58 060 kg. And so on.

A Flight Plan with a constant consumption but varying TAS is somewhat more involved; the plan must be done line by line, and the estimation of weights to find a mean TAS has its hazards, since no times on the legs are available.

A snippet from the data:

Consumption	Mean Weight (kg) v. TAS (kt)			
kg/hr	79 000	77 000	74 000	72 000
2 400	300	308	319	326

Weight at commencement of climb: 81 000 kg
Climb: Mean TAS 235 kt, time 48 min, fuel used 2 250 kg

The climb leg can be solved for G/S, time, distance and the rest, and the weight at start of level flight is 78 750 kg.

Without a G/S or time for the next leg, one can only look at the distance, glance at the data, and extract visually a likely TAS; obtain from this TAS and the forecast W/V a rough G/S; with this G/S, get an approximate time for the leg; halve it, and suggest a fuel used by mid-leg; and thereby calculate a mean weight.

Thus:

Weight at start 78 750 kg, next leg 190 nm
W/V 140/35, Track 210(T).
Try TAS 305 kt; this gives G/S 290 kt.

Total suggested time: 39 min therefore

Mid-time = 20 min
20 min at 2 400 kg/hr = 800 kg
∴ Mean weight = 77 950 kg

Use this weight to extract the TAS from the table = 304 kt and complete the leg of the Flight Plan. The actual fuel used will be 1 560 kg. Check. The weight at start of next leg is 77 190 kg, whence to continue the exercise.

On finishing the final line to destination, the fuel used from departure to destination can be totted up (Item A), as well as the weight over the destination field at some specified altitude; this weight, less any fuel used for descent and landing, will give the anticipated landing weight.

In calculating the fuel or TAS for the alternate from the data given, it is sufficient to use the weight at start of descent as a leader into the requirements for the leg.

The fuel to destination plus alternate fuel plus contingency fuel plus taxi, takeoff, circuit, landing plus any other reserves or percentages will give the total fuel required for the trip; from this figure, the payload can be worked out, and this is what keeps us in business.

All this, the type of Flight Plan in qualifying exams for pilot licences, may have astounded you in its vagaries and guesswork; have no fear, it is but a presentation of the principles of the stuff to the student pilot: the manuals are of course much more precise, full of information garnered from tests and checks carried out with care and accuracy, but still on mean weights as shown, though for a specified period of time. We will move on to this practical matter at once.

Presentation of Data

Every aircraft type produces a cruise control manual, wherein all information at all heights at all temperatures for each specific purpose is shown, either graphically or tabulated, the latter by far the more popular. Climb, short range diversion, level cruise by appropriate methods, 4-engines, 3-engines, 2-engines, level cruise; in fact anything that the pilot requires for his aircraft for his route, presented succinctly, for rapid production of the Flight Plan with the station manager breathing down his neck to get him away, the fuel wallah palpitating for the fuel requirements, the load people agitating for pay load particulars. You won't get the aircraft type on your licence till you've mastered the manual, but for examination purposes, the Civil Aviation Authority has produced some Data Sheets set out along the accepted lines. Data Sheets 33 are part of your equipment, so we'll refer to them constantly and work out a Flight Plan sample.

First, though, an understanding of a primary problem is necessary. A pilot is mainly required to fly at a Pressure Altitude, simply an altitude with 1013·2 mb set on the sub-scale, but the aircraft's performance is vitally affected by the density of the atmosphere it is flying in, the TAS increasing for a given power as the density decreases: thus, density altitude is the operative altitude, – the pressure altitude corrected for temperature.

In the tables, you will see that in the right hand top corner of each sheet is the temperature square covered by that particular table, noted in relation to standard; the standard of +15°C at mean sea level, pressure 1013·2 mb, decreasing at 1·98°C per 1 000 feet, and the rest. This square contains the temperature deviation. To avoid undue strain on the pilot's grey matter, on page 33F, the standard temperatures at all pressure altitudes to 42 000 ft are set out. The relation of the forecast temperature at required altitude to standard can thus readily be obtained, and the appropriate sheet used for the Flight Plan.

Let us now plough gently through the following Flight Plan, assisted by Data Sheets 33: remember the penalties are heavy for violent arithmetical inaccuracies in the exam as well as in the air: – you would feel a real charley to find in mid trip that you'd uplifted 1 000 kg too little fuel.

Information is as follows:

A flight is to be made from ROME TO ACCRA. LAGOS is the terminal alternate. Route details are given on the pro forma.

Loading:	Weight at start of take-off is 130 000 kg.
Climb:	Climb on track from 1 000 ft over ROME to flight level 340. (Table 33A).
Cruise:	Cruise at the levels given in the Flight Plan (Table 33C).
Descent:	Descend on Track to arrive over ACCRA at 1 000 ft. (Table 33E).
Alternate:	Use Table 33G. Assume diversion is commenced 1 000 ft over ACCRA and ends at 1 000 ft over LAGOS.
Fuel: (i)	Sufficient for take-off and climb to 1 000 ft over ROME, plus:
(ii)	Sufficient for flight from ROME to ACCRA and to alternate LAGOS, plus:

FLIGHT PLAN

STAGE From	STAGE To	Flight Level	Temp. Dev. °C	WIND Direction	WIND Speed kt.	Track °(T)	Drift	Heading °(T)	T.A.S. kt.	Wind comp. kt.	G.S kt.	Distance n.m.	Time min.	Fuel flow kg./hr.	Wt. at start Kg.	Fuel required Kg.
	TAKE OFF FUEL															
ROME	Top of climb		− 3	040	20	170										
Top of climb	PALERMO	340	+ 2	340	50	170						244		—		
PALERMO	IDRIS	350	+ 4	290	70	180						331				
IDRIS	GHAT	350	+ 4	310	50	198						490				
GHAT	NIAMY	350	+ 8	280	80	213						824				
NIAMY	Top of descent	350	+12	210	15	197						487				
Top of descent	ACCRA		—	200	10	197			—		—			—		
ACCRA	LAGOS		—	200	20	075						217		—		

FLIGHT PLAN

STAGE From	STAGE To	Flight Level	Temp. Dev. °C	WIND Direction	WIND Speed kt.	Track °(T)	Drift	Heading °(T)	T.A.S. kt.	Wind comp. kt.	G/S kt.	Distance n.m.	Time min.	Fuel flow kg./hr.	Wt. at start 130000 Kg.	Fuel required Kg.
	TAKE OFF FUEL	↓							↓			↑	02	→	129000 →	1000
ROME	Top of climb	(climb)	−3	040	20	170	2S	168	379	+14	393	131	20	—	124600	4400
Top of climb	PALERMO	340	+2	340	50	170	1P	171	488	+49	537	113 (244)	12¼	7050	123130	1470
PALERMO	IDRIS	350	+4	290	70	180	8P	188	486	+20	506	331	39½	6900	118530	4600
IDRIS	GHAT	350	+4	310	50	198	6P	204	486	+17	503	490	58½	6710	111980	6550
GHAT	NIAMY	350	+8	280	80	213	9P	222	486	−36	450	824	1.50	6450	100190	11790
NIAMY	Top of descent	350	+12	210	15	197	0	197	494	−15	479	394 (487)	49½	6115	95140	5050
Top of descent	ACCRA	(descent)	—	200	10	197	0	197	369	−10	559	93	15½	—	94440	7000
															Item A	5560
ACCRA	LAGOS	(climb/descent)	—	200	20	075	21	077	—	+12	—	217	35	—		3730

(iii)   800 kg for circuit and landing, plus:

(iv)   9 000 kg reserve

    (a) Complete the Flight Plan.

    (b) What weight of fuel is required?

Before starting, note that computer work is reduced by Drift and Wind Component Tables, pages 24 and 25 of the Data Sheet leaflet. The TAS is regarded broadly to give sufficient accuracy for flight planning purposes: a set is provided for each aircraft, with its mean cruising speed, mean climb and mean diversion speed. Here we have two tables, 480 kt and 380 kt; the wind speed is set out across the top, with the angle between wind direction and Track down the side. Thus, a drift and wind component can be read off, though the port or starboard bit must be determined. Thus, Track 180(T), W/V 290/70, your expected TAS 486 kt — angle is 110° down the side, against wind speed 70, drift is 8, component +20; use G/S 506 kt, and with a southerly Track with rough westerly wind, drift is clearly port. The appropriate table can be used to press on with the Flight Plan.

Wrinkle number 1 is to put your weight at start of take-off, 130 000 kg, on top of the column. On Table 33A, four engined climb, on the sheet labelled 'Standard −5°C to −1°C' in the right hand corner, −3 being the temp dev from standard, mean for the climb. The notes on the bottom are very pertinent; so take-off fuel to 1 000 ft is 1 000 kg, time 2 min, which can be filled in on the Flight Plan: the weight at the start of the next leg is thus 129 000 kg, but this is filled in on the 'Take-off fuel' line.

Climb

To make it easier, the actual TOW is along the top, the pressure height at the side. Along the height 34 000 to climb to, read off TAS 379 kt, and continue along to the 130 000 kg TOW column, read off fuel consumed 4 400 kg, time 20 min, and enter in: weight at start of next leg, now 124 600, and the line can be completed, including a distance of 131 nm, leaving 113 nm to go from top of climb to PALERMO. Check.

Level

All the time the temp dev and FL must be watched: there is absolutely no reason why one shouldn't move from one page to another. And as an obiter dictum; Flight Level is the same thing as Pressure Height. Here we go to Table 33C, Standard 0 to +9°C. The top line is separated into individual hours of cruise, and the side has again pressure height and mean TAS: if you started at 137 000 kg, at 34 000 ft and flew at that pressure height, provided the temperature did not go outside the limits for the table, one could go steadily along the line. In this case, our weight at start is 124 600 kg, at 34 000 ft, TAS is straight 488 kt, but we must interpolate for fuel flow between the column:

$$129 : 7\,300 \text{ and } 122 : 6\,900$$

The columnar weight difference is 7 000 kg for a consumption difference of 400 kg

So: $124\,600 - 122\,000 = 2\,600$

$$\frac{2\,600}{7\,000} \times 400 \text{ gives } 150 \text{ kg to the nearest } 10 \text{ kg}$$

∴ consumption for 124 600 kg initial weight
is $6\,900 + 150 = 7\,050$ kg

which enter, and complete the PALERMO line, and be careful where you enter the fuel required of 1 470 kg (that's what you made it, I hope). The biggest boobs in Flight Planning are invariably arithmetical, cocking up a thousand with a hundred digit.

Proceed now with a start weight of 123 130 kg to IDRIS, checking the temp dev, O.K., keep the same page: but the pressure height is now 35 000 ft. From the notes on page 2 of the Data Sheets, an en route climb of 4 000 ft is ignored for time, but add 200 kg to fuel used: to be perfect then, we need to chuck in 50 kg to the fuel required on the IDRIS leg for a 1 000 ft climb. From Table 33C, TAS 486 kt, and 6 900 kg is accurate enough for 123 130 kg weight at start. Complete the line, and you'll find $39\frac{1}{2}$ min gives you 4 550 kg required, +50 kg, a round 4 600. Weight at start for GHAT 118 530 kg. Into the Tables again, check the temp dev, O.K. Interpolate as before, between 123 : 6 900 kg and 116 : 6 600 kg for a consumption at 118 500 kg aircraft weight.

$$\frac{2\,500}{7\,000} \times 300 = \frac{750}{7} = 110 \text{ kg}$$

to be added to the 116 000 weight consumption = 6 710 kg, and the TAS is still 486 kt.

Complete the GHAT and NIAMY lines. We now must deal with the descent line to find time and distance covered before we can find out how far along the Track NIAMY — ACCRA to fly before commencing the descent. This is Table 33E, and is as plain as a pikestaff: as we're leaving 35 000 ft, TAS is 369 kt, fuel used 700 kg, time $15\frac{1}{2}$ min. Complete the descent line, enter distances for the level and descent bits, and now to finish off NIAMY — TOD: the temp dev is +12°C, so with a weight at start of 100 190 kg on the table marked 'Standard +10°C to +14°C', enter at 35 000 ft, TAS 494 kt, interpolate for 100 000 kg between 103 : 6 200 and 96 : 6 000, giving 115 kg to add to 6 000, giving 6 115 kg consumption. Finish off so far: add the fuel requirements from departure to destination, usually known as Item A, and above all check that your weight at ACCRA + this figure = 130 000 kg.

The alternate must now be dealt with, Table 33G. The explanatory notes are reasonably clear: enter the tables for your conditions, and then make corrections. We're at 1 000 ft, will climb to 35 000 ft and descend to arrive over LAGOS at 1 000 ft. From drift and wind component table for TAS 380 kt, extract drift 2P, wind component +12, enter 33G and with a spot of visual interpolation: 35 min, 3 620 kg. Corrections are: none for height, weight is 94 400 kg ∴ add 3%, 108 kg say 110, used 3 730 kg. The corrections are all straightforward, and they are set out for you: no need to learn them by heart; it is automatic to check them, though, in every Flight Plan.

All that needs be done now is to tot up the Fuel on Board requirements, as demanded by the question, or by the Station Officer on the route. It is wise to set it out as on a fuel chit.

Item A	35 560
Alternate	3 730
Circuit & Landing	800
Reserve	9 000
FOB	49 090 kg

This makes it easy to deduce the landing weight at ACCRA, for example: you will use the 800 kg for circuit and landing, but still have alternate and reserve fuel in the tanks.

Divers problems in Flight Planning (Data Sheets 33)
The quite practical type of problem that involves a trip of a certain distance, part at low altitude (29 000 ft or below), part at high, hold and descend, is straightforward once you know your way around the Data Sheets. The information presented to you in an examination or in the Briefing Room must be complete enough for an answer to be arrived at, and there should be no difficulty, for example, in working out a descent before solving the time and fuel for cruise: there's nothing new in that. Table 33E for descent couldn't really be easier. I'm not trying to offend your intelligence in reminding you that a hold is a hold, where a ground speed is unnecessary: in the artificial atmosphere of the exam room, it is easy to start hunting for the absurd like 'how far have I gone on the hold leg'.

Table 33D gives the Low Level Cruise information, and do, oh do, notice the footnote about the mean weight of 100 000 kg. A mean weight of 135 000 kg increases the consumption at 15 000 ft at ISA +7, by 705 kg/hr. The table otherwise is self explanatory, calling for only the simplest interpolation.

A climb from 15 000 ft to 34 000 ft in Table 33A demands a simple subtraction of fuel at 15 000 ft for the weight at start of climb from the fuel at 34 000 ft, but a visual interpolation is required at bottom and top for intermediate weights. Keeping ISA +7, with a weight of 133 840 kg at 15 000 ft to start the climb to 34 000 ft, the table says —

Press Height	Mean TAS	135 000 kg		130 000 kg	
		Fuel kg	Time min	Fuel kg	Time min
34 000	387	5 800	31	5 300	28
15 000	324	2 100	9	2 000	9

Fuel at 15 000 ft for 133 840 kg aircraft weight is 2 080 kg
Fuel at 34 000 ft for 133 840 kg aircraft weight is 5 700 kg
Fuel used for this climb, then, is 3 620 kg, and such a round-off figure is quite adequate, as is the similarly subtractive time of 22 min.

The mean TAS for this climb demands an entry into the graph labelled for the exercise as Table 33B: enter with top of climb height across to the appropriate start of climb height curve, drop to the Reference line, and then parallel up or down as far as the temp dev axis, and read off the mean TAS. Our example above gives 418 kt. Interpolation of the bottom of climb curve is visually done. Don't make a large theoretical chore of any of this: the table, anyway, gives an example, which is worth a moment's study.

Descent is plain sailing (Table 33E) just read off TAS, fuel used and time taken from altitude to 1 000 ft: if the bottom of descent is not 1 000 ft, subtract one fuel from t'other, ditto time; add the two TAS and subtract 290. Hold is taken at the altitude on Table 33D, and the fuel calculated for the time of hold.

Try this, using Data Sheets No. 33

An aircraft is to fly from A to B, a distance of 950 nm on a Track of 250(T). Take-off weight is 140 000 kg, and the aircraft will successively:

(i)   Climb from 1 000 ft to 15 000 ft, and then cruise at this level for 25 min.

(ii)   Climb from 15 000 ft to 34 000 ft and cruise at this level until a descent is made to arrive over B at 6 000 ft.

(iii)   Hold at 6 000 ft over B for 30 min (Table 33D) and then descend over B to 1 000 ft.

Details of these stages, temp dev and W/V are given below.

Complete the Flight Plan, giving the total fuel required and the total time.

STAGE Press Alt	Temp Dev	W/V	TAS	Wind Com- ponent	G/S	Dist	Time min	Fuel Flow kg/hr	Start Weight kg	Fuel kg
T/O & climb to 1 000 ft	–	–	–	–	–	–		–		
1 000 – 15 000 ft	+3	200/40						–		
Level 15 000 ft	+6	240/50					25			
15 000 – 34 000 ft	+6	260/60						–		
Level 34 000 ft	+8	290/70								
34 000 – 6 000 ft	–	230/50						–		
Hold at 6 000 ft	+6	–			–	–	30			
6 000 – 1 000 ft	–	–		–	–	–		–		
	·					950				

Answer: 24 000 kg; 3 h 02 m.

The following problem is really an exercise in figure manipulation and logical method, but it has a very practical role, for often the weight of the aircraft at destination is the limiting factor.

Using Data Sheets No. 33, a flight is to be made from A to B, distance 1 150 nm, to arrive over B at 6 000 ft at weight 98 000 kg

Climb   On Track from 1 000 ft over A to FL 340 (Temp dev +6, head wind component 30 kt)

Cruise   Four-engine level cruise at 0.86 Mach at FL 340 (Temp dev +6, head wind component 55 kt)

Descent   On Track to arrive over B at 6 000 ft (head wind component 25 kt)

Give the time and fuel required for:

(i)   Climb from 1 000 ft

(ii)   Cruise

(iii)   Descent

Descent first, from Table 33E:

TAS $(367 + 300) - 290 = 377$ kt:

$\therefore$ G/S is 352 kt. Time given 12 min, so distance 70 nm:

Fuel given 600 kg:

Weight at start of descent is therefore 98 600 kg.

Level next, Table 33C, temp dev +6°C:

TAS 488 kt $\therefore$ G/S 433 kt.

The aircraft's weight is going to finish the cruise sector at 98 600 kg; in the Table, from 102 000 to 98 600 kg gives:

Fuel 3 400 kg.

At noted consumption of 6 200 kg/hr, this takes 33 min:

33 min at G/S 433 kt gives distance 238 nm

The next hour uses 6 400 kg and distance 433 nm

A mental check indicates that there may be little cruise distance left, so take a summary:

After the climb and an undetermined period of cruise, the all-up-weight is:

98 000 + 600 + 3 400 + 6 400 = 108 400 kg

Similarly, the distance gone is:

1 150 − (70 + 238 + 433) = 409 nm

To enter the climb table, the TOW is required, so this must at this stage be estimated as accurately as possible. A glance at the appropriate page of Table 33A suggests a 22 min climb at a TOW of 115 000 kg, fuel used 4 300 kg; the climb G/S 357 kt for this time means 131 nm will be covered on the climb, and 278 nm is left for the very first cruise bit. Continuing with this procedure, enter the level cruise Table, read off the consumption 6 700 kg/hr, calculate the time to do 278 nm at G/S 433 kt; thus, $38\frac{1}{2}$ min and fuel used 4 300 kg. The approximate TOW is:

108 400 + 4 300 + 4 300 = 117 000 kg,

and although the climb table gives fuel and time from 1 000 ft which is just what the question demands, the top line is classified as TOW and 1 000 kg must be included in the TOW figure for the initial take-off climb. Entering the table then with 118 000 kg:

Climb takes 23 min, uses 4 500 kg, distance 137 nm. Level flight starts at 112 500 kg all-up-weight (the initial climb fuel of 1 000 kg being allowed for), and so this portion will take 38 min to fly the 272 nm at G/S 433 kt, at fuel consumption 6 600 kg/hr = 4 200 kg. There is an element of meaning-off the extracted figures from the entered figures in the tables for intermediate weights, but there is no need for pedantic precision.

The answers are:
  (i)   Climb: 23 min, fuel 4 500 kg
  (ii) Cruise: 2h 11m, fuel 14 000 kg
  (iii) Descent: 12 min, fuel 600 kg

Diversion and Hold

Another practical problem in this paper is a diversion arranged for you somewhere in the closing stages of a trip. As the examiner wants to know if you are really familiar with the tables, he will divert you half way down the descent, and give you a hold. At one fell swoop, he's got you in every table in the book, and a good thing too. Since a diversion is assumed to be demanded after a shot at landing which has proved out of the question, diversion tables have overshoot, climb to a suitable level, reserve fuel all included in the figures; to peel off on the way down and head for the alternate field must require suitable corrections to these figures. In Data sheets 33 these corrections are clearly shown, but in sheets 34 they are not, and circumstances will decide which of the more thumbed tables are appropriate in the latter case, not forgetting the Low Level Cruise set.

Perhaps it's opportune to take a look at Data sheets 34; these are geared for heavier aircraft, but are similar in format, and mainly self-explanatory, though watch the footnotes as before. Interpolations for fuel consumption between stated weights are definitely only to the nearest 100 kg, and the Low Level cruise table is the one to use if holding.

An aircraft cruising at 0.83 indicated Mach at 34 000 ft pressure height is on Track to destination B which is 640 nm distant. Aircraft weight is 238 500 kg, temp dev +7°C, headwind component 40 kt.

Later, descent on Track is commenced, headwind component 20 kt.
(a) Give the time and fuel required for:
    (i) Cruise
    (ii) Descent

The aircraft arrives at B, but diverts after an overshoot to D, 156 nm distant, tailwind component 30 kt, temp dev +8°C.
(b) Give the aircraft weight at commencement of diversion.
(c) Determine time, flight level, and fuel required for diversion.

The aircraft holds over D at FL 160 for 17 min, temp dev +14 (Table 34D).
(d) Give the fuel required for holding.

Descent   14½ min, 2 000 kg, TAS 372 kt, from Table 34E
          ∴ G/S 352 kt, distance run 85 nm.

Cruise   which will be for 555 nm
          TAS 486 kt, ∴ G/S 446 kt, time 1 hr 14½ min

AUW 238 500 kg

          so in Table 34C, temp dev +7°C, interpolate for weight and height to give
          fuel flow 9 700 kg/hr for the first hour, and 9 500 kg/hr for the second.
          Cruise fuel: 1 hr   9 700
                       14½ min   2 300
                          Total   12 000 kg
    Answer (a) (i) 1 hr 14½ min, 12 000 kg
                 (ii) 14½ min, 2 000 kg

Now for the diversion; fuel used to B is 14 000 kg, and the aircraft weight after overshoot is 238 500 − 14 000 = 224 500 kg.

Entering Table 34B, interpolate for 156 nm and a 30 kt tailwind, read fuel 13 900 kg, FL 220, time 31 min. The start of diversion weight is 30 500 kg less than tabulated, so footnote correction (a) must be applied; this is 6% of 13 900, subtractive, 800 kg, = 13 100 kg.

    Answer (b)   224 500 kg
            (c)   31 min, FL 220, 13 100 kg.

For the hold, TAS 434 kt is extracted from the Table 34D, but the fuel flow must be checked against aircraft weight as per the footnote. Diversion started at 224 500 kg AUW, and 13 100 kg was to be used; this figure contains 7 500 kg reserve, and the aircraft has descended only to FL 160. Of the actual fuel required, 5 600 kg (13 100 − 7 500), the amount unused at the hold point would be the descent from FL 160 to landing, a figure of 1 800 kg from the descent table. A round estimate of what fuel has in fact been burnt off would be 3 800 kg, and the AUW at holding 220 700 kg. Thus, the noted consumption of 12 500 kg in the Table is satisfactory, and the correction element is not applicable.

    Answer (d)   17 min at 12 500 kg/hr = 3 550 kg.

This example has put you into the diversion table, but if the descent had been broken off, say, at FL 180, whence to proceed direct to the alternate, then the calculations must be made from the descent, climb and cruise tables, starting from the AUW at the time of break off; since the diversion table showed that FL 220 would be climbed to, then from FL 180 a climb to around FL 340 would be possible and advisable.

Just to make sure you're not betting on avoiding a question on 3-engine operation, take a look at Table 34G in Data sheets 34 for such a problem as the following.

An aircraft en route to K goes on 3 engines at 1307.

Descent will be made on Track. Details are:

Distance	926 nm
Track	123(T)
Mean W/V	180/60
FL	310
Temp dev	+8°C

Aircraft weight at 1307 is 235 700 kg

Fuel in tanks at 1307 is 41 300 kg

(a)   Give ETA K

(b)   How much fuel remaining on landing?

<u>Descent</u> first: TAS 358 kt, fuel 1 900 kg, time 14 min

∴ G/S 322 kt, distance 75 nm, and cruise distance is then 851 nm.

AUW 235 700 kg, mean TAS 451 kt, 9 700 kg/hr at first, from the appropriate section of Table 34G.

∴ G/S 418 kt, time 2 hr 02 min

<u>Fuel</u>	first hour	9 700 kg
	second hour	9 200 kg
	02 min	300 kg, this calculated at 9 000 kg/hr to be precise, but it becomes pedantic in this case
	Cruise fuel	19 200 kg
	+Descent fuel	1 900 kg
	Total used	21 100 kg

This total subtracted from fuel available at 1307 gives 20 200 kg left on landing.

ETA 1307 + 2 hr 02 cruise + 14 min descent = 1523 hrs

<u>Answer</u>   (a)   ETA K 1523

(b)   20 200 kg.

Quite straightforward, providing you have familiarity. As a rider, the 3-engine cruise in our favourite Data Sheets 33, Table 33H, is set out page by page for temp dev from standard, giving TAS at height and consumption per hour for a given weight at start: descent would call for normal descent Table 33E. Take a look at it right now or you'll be sorry.

To sum up for the Flight Plan itself, and such matters just discussed, you will need to do some of the published exam papers to get up some reasonable speed with accuracy: there is no need to be pedantic about fuel consumption. For instance, the tables themselves are not precise to a couple of hundred kilos — a weight of 101 100 kg gives a consumption 6 400 kg/hr and the following hour the AUW at start is 95 000 kg. There is a lot of averaging out, and though precision is always to be aimed for, it must be reasonable. You will find too the Drift and Wind Component table at the end of the book helps speed things along, using the appropriate table for the climb or level: all that computer work is avoided. The failing point in Flight Planning is pure arithmetical error, frequently induced by examination neurosis.

9: Choice of Route

On an Airline running schedule services, it would appear at first sight that the Captain has precious little say: certainly the majority of local trips around the UK to the European continent are fixed on an airways route at pre-arranged altitudes, and fortunately for pilot morale, however much they may appear to resemble a taxi service, the vagaries of weather and the need to practise all types of let-downs are ever present. On long routes, despite the firm establishment of various different tracks across the water or desert, the Captain must study the overall weather picture at selected heights and pick the best route for speed, the best height for his particular aircraft under the conditions, never forgetting passenger comfort (or animal comfort if he's carrying a load of monkeys), viewing the whole thing with an eye on fuel consumption and safety at all times. This takes some expertise to do briskly and surely, and while there is nothing worse than the type who hums and ha's muttering 'ye canna be too careful', it is positively better than the impulsive one who decides too quickly and pours his 100 ton flying cigar into turbulent weather away from operating navigation aids.

The scheduled services are but a part of the Airline picture: any number of firms specialise in charter operations, and the majority are prepared to do charters, hiring aircraft if necessary from their competitors. Immediately, the profit motive could incite the Captain to take undue risks, especially if he is recently promoted to command and is anxious to make a name for himself as a good company man. Happily, by the time he is ready for such elevation, he has learnt more sense, apart from the legislative exercises he has had to undergo.

In such operations, the route and height are his decision: he will have in good time pondered the variables, and be ready at the Met briefing with a selection of possible routes from which to make a quick and safe choice; in fact, he may already have decided from his bedside after a chat with the met man and the operations chap, so that on arrival at the field the Flight Plan is prepared and he needs only to check and corroborate that the latest information confirms his previous telephone briefing.

The procedure hardly varies; knowing his aircraft's heights for optimum operation, power- and fuel-wise, he will view a route first which will give him the best time track, examine it for trappy forecasts of turbulence or icing; for nav aids en route; for active danger areas notified for the time on the Notams; for Air Traffic Control restrictions and requirements; for safe clearance of topographical obstacles. Can he get over the highest mountains en route at the weight he will be at the time he gets there? Not only over them, but well over them? The broad decision now taken, he must at once examine the forecast weather at destination and departure field and at suitable alternates; not only alternates at his destination, but at the departure point, in case of return. Is there an en route aerodrome available for landing if the destination clamps, thereby avoiding a possible diversion to some destination alternate when fuel is getting low, and the destination alternate is suffering from the same foul weather as the destination itself? Is a chosen alternate not only far enough away from the clamped destination to be reached comfortably with the fuel aboard, forecast OK for weather, but also politically OK for the passengers and crew to be allowed through immigration in the case of a long wait? Is the required type of fuel available there? Are the takeoff and landing conditions restrictive? Are the necessary services available there at the possible arrival time? The world is scattered with airfields which do not fill all these requirements, only useful in case of force majeure.

The next check is on TOW and landing conditions: at expected TOW will the met conditions allow a safe unstick? With that TOW, less the expected fuel consumption from departure to destination (Item A + oil and water used, + extra required for climb, taxi, T/O, circuit and landing), is the maximum landing weight greater than the maximum allowed for the aircraft or by the airfield itself? If so, will the fuel uplift be reduced to allow a safe operation? Or shall the payload be reduced?

He can now address himself to cruise control and fuel: long range cruise, or constant power, depending on whether fuel conservation is more important than speed, or whether speed is possible with no fuel problems. All aircraft manufacturers produce their tables, and a little experience of their operation makes the decision more or less immediate. With the Item A + fuel required for alternate (latter usually at Long Range Cruise) he now considers his reserves, bearing in mind all the previous factors mentioned. A Route Contingency reserve is usually laid down by the Company, a percentage of Item A, with a maximum amount: this allows for the hard trip when actual winds are more adverse than forecast or for any of those happenings which are part of the flying game, such as being ordered to fly at an unsatisfactory altitude for the aircraft, or to move off Flight Planned Track for any reason, weather or traffic. The amount of contingency fuel is normally determined by the route: over country plentifully supplied with good airfields, the percentage of Item A would not be so large as that over the oceans or deserts. A similar percentage is usually applied to the alternate fuel, and for the same reasons. An emergency reserve is frequently added for Mother, + a goodly quantity for stand off, climb out, and taxi, the amount depending on the aircraft, and the complexity of the traffic at destination. It is almost normal in dodgy weather to have a stack of 20 aircraft at a place like NEW YORK, and plaintive cries from pilots that fuel is low and precedence is required are viewed very palely indeed from the other poor devils holding at precise altitudes for hours on end.

The only likely major difference to this type of routine will be if the destination is an island set solitary-like in the silver sea, a hearty distance from another aerodrome. Then, once having passed the Point of No Return, or the latest time to divert to a suitable field on the beam of Track, and a landing at destination becomes obligatory, an Island Reserve is substituted for alternate fuel, reserve fuel, and stand off fuel, to permit a long hold.

Add the lot up, and that's the Load Sheet Fuel: an Endurance is worked out from this from a graph or a rule of thumb average to give the maximum time the aircraft can be airborne.

Sundry wrinkles will become apparent, nearly all allowed for in the Aircraft Type Manual. The total fuel on board may include a quantity of unusable fuel in the tanks:

the only interest in this for the operation is that it's part of the weight. Climb, taxi, take-off fuel will be laid down in the Manual, and included on the Flight Plan; en route climb and allowances for it will be considered in the body of the Flight Plan from an appropriate table or graph; fuel for heaters, de-icers and so on are similarly allowed for. One pretty point often overlooked especially on shortish sectors is to jug up to the gills with fuel where the price is cheap, or to take the minimum consonant with safety where it is high: this will endear you to the commercial side of the company, for the savings can be appreciable.

10: Weight Calculation

Being in an international business the pilot is constantly plagued with units different from the ones he's been brought up on, and despite efforts to bring them all to one acceptable type world-wide, there's always the nation which won't confer or won't agree. In general, kilograms are becoming the accepted weight unit, though the pilot will find pounds aplenty on the trips. Volume should thus be in litres, and this comes hard to many, used to Imperial gallons. The U.S. gallon is only about 4/5 of the Imperial gallon, so there's another snag. It is quite unnecessary to memorise the conversion units, they're all on the computer anyway or in the Flight Manual, but when dealing with large figures, you should have an approximate idea of the relationship in order to get the number of noughts correct.

     1 kilogram is 2·2 lb
     1 litre is about 1/5th Imperial gallon
     1 litre is about 1/3rd of a U.S. gallon

     The weight of fuel varies with temperature and air density, as it will according to its octane value: the conversion from volume occupied (i.e. litres or gallons) to weight (kg or lb) is found by knowing the fuel's specific gravity at the time of loading. An engineer will have used his hygrometer to find this, and the sum is simple. It must of course be entered on the Load Sheet; on the Flight Plan, weight is the only concern.

     The specific gravity is simply the relation of the weight of fuel at the time for a given volume to the weight of water for the same volume.

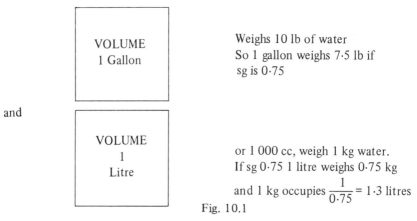

VOLUME 1 Gallon — Weighs 10 lb of water So 1 gallon weighs 7·5 lb if sg is 0·75

and

VOLUME 1 Litre — or 1 000 cc, weigh 1 kg water. If sg 0·75 1 litre weighs 0·75 kg and 1 kg occupies $\frac{1}{0.75} = 1.3$ litres

Fig. 10.1

The circular slide rule works all this out for you, and you will see that kg to lb is straightforward, but you cannot convert litres to kg, gals to lb, or any variant of these without knowing the sg — the errors can be considerable, and there must be no guesswork at all.

The precautions to be observed with respect to maximum TOW and maximum landing weight after obtaining total fuel requirements have already been mentioned; the fuel requirements, although calculated with precision, are the minimum requirements for safe operation, for there would be no point in lugging excess fuel around; thence, the payload carried must be such that these maxima are not exceeded, and off-loading passengers or freight is a serious decision in a commercial concern. But just as maxima are laid down for aircraft weight, so for each flight there must be a maximum payload that can be carried.

Consider the following example:

Maximum TOW 250 000 kg
Maximum Landing Weight 190 000 kg
Weight without Fuel or Payload 170 000 kg
Fuel on Board 23 535 kg
Fuel required from departure to destination 16 535 kg

The point to start with is Max Ldg Wt 190 000 kg. The only difference between this imperative maximum and the actual TOW is the fuel used up from departure to destination, the 'burn-off'.

So 190 000 kg
    16 535

    206 535   is the TOW

This is well below the maximum TOW, but dare not be exceeded, for if it was, the aircraft would be above maximum landing weight at the destination and would be forced to chunter around simply to use fuel and get the weight down.

The weight without fuel or payload, 170 000 kg, may now be added to the total fuel on board to give 193 535 kg, the weight without payload. Then 206 535 − 193 535 = 13 000 kg payload, pretty poor for such a heavy aircraft, but when going to spots like Iceland, calling for much fuel for an alternate in Scotland, such a case can frequently happen.

Another then:

Maximum TOW 47 300 kg
Weight less fuel and payload 33 400 kg
Fuel required from departure to destination 9 775 kg
Reserve fuel (assume unused) 1 985 kg

What is maximum payload that can be carried?
47 300 − 33 400 = 13 900 kg = fuel + payload.
FOB is 9 775 + 1 985 = 11 760 kg
∴ Payload is 2 140 kg

All the problems boil down to either of these types, and in practice the Station Duty Officer has a simple form to resolve them. The 'burn-off' will usually include not only the fuel used from departure to destination but also oil and water.

Regulated landing weight	52 618 kg	Max TOW under forecast
Burn-off	18 240	conditions 72 575
	70 858 kg	

RTOW	70 858 kg
Estimated weight, no fuel (Empty Tank weight)	42 628
Max Fuel Available	28 230 kg
Flight Plan Fuel	28 230 kg
Excess Available	NIL
Loadsheet Fuel	28 230 kg
+ Taxi and etc.	500
This is the fuel in your tanks	28 730 kg TOW 70 858 kg

And you will see that the restricting factor on this trip was landing weight, and the fuel uplifted exactly the Flight Plan requirements.

To sum up

The restriction invariably is Maximum TOW or Maximum Landing weight, and keep in mind that the difference between actual TOW and actual Ldg wt is the fuel consumed on the leg. With the colossal payloads carried nowadays, the huge expenses involved in commercial airline operations, and the alleged tight margins on which these undertakings struggle to show a profit, all being signs of a cut-throat price war, it follows that economy on every trip will be more vital than ever. Though much of the paper work is done in the office, the captain and crew must be able to check it all quickly and thoroughly, safety being the only factor to override commercial stringency. A few further worked examples will not come amiss, and the CAA for sure realise their importance, if you get our meaning.

Example 1

A simple revision example, for a start:

Load sheet data is as follows:

Max Ldg wt 139 550 kg

A/c weight without fuel or payload 90 000 kg

Reserve fuel (assume unused) 3 000 kg

Max TOW 167 000 kg

Time to destination 3 hr 33 min

Time from destination to alternate 51 min

Fuel consumption 2 500 kg/hr

What is TOW, and maximum payload that can be carried?

Answer   3 hr 33 min + 51 min = 4 hr 24 min @ 2500 kg/hr = 11 000 kg
                + reserve 3000 kg = FOB 14 000 kg.

Fuel for the leg to destination:

3 hr 33 min @ 2 500 kg/hr = 8 880 kg,

Now	Ldg wt	139 550 kg max
	Burn off	8 880 kg
∴	TOW	148 430 kg

a/c wt, no fuel, no payload	90 000 kg
FOB	+ 14 000 kg
a/c wt, no payload	104 000 kg

so	148 430 kg TOW, actual
	−104 000 kg
∴ PAYLOAD	44 430 kg

Example 2

A/c weight without fuel or payload	40 000 kg
Max Ldg wt	49 550 kg
Route fuel, excluding reserve	12 890 kg
Reserve fuel	1 650 kg

Assuming reserve fuel is unused, determine,
  (a) Maximum payload which can be carried.
  (b) TOW with this maximum payload.

Answer

Ldg wt	49 550 kg	a/c wt, no fuel, no payload	40 000 kg
Fuel used	12 890 kg	FOB	12 890 kg
			+ 1 650 kg
TOW	62 440 kg		
		Wt, no payload	54 540 kg

TOW	62 440 kg
Wt, no payload	−54 540 kg
∴ PAYLOAD	7 900 kg

Example 3

This example involves both types.
Load sheet reads:

A/c wt, no fuel, no payload	63 200 kg
Max TOW	99 000 kg
Route fuel (excluding reserve)	18 200 kg
Reserve (assume unused)	3 000 kg

  (a) Give payload for a maximum TOW.
If max Ldg wt is 76 500 kg, determine
  (b) TOW when maximum payload is carried.
  (c) Maximum payload.

Answer

(a)	Wt, no fuel, no payload	63 200 kg
	Route fuel	18 200 kg
	Reserve fuel	+ 3 000 kg
	Wt, no payload	84 400 kg
	Max TOW	99 000 kg
	Wt, no payload	−84 400 kg
	PAYLOAD	14 600 kg

(b)	Max Ldg wt	76 500 kg	(c)	TOW	94 700 kg
	Route fuel	+18 200 kg		Wt, no payload	−84 400 kg
	TOW	94 700 kg		PAYLOAD	10 300 kg

Example 4

You are to fly from P to Q where your fuel is not available, and return to P: a maximum payload is to be off-loaded at Q, and a maximum payload uplifted there. The following are the pertinent data:

Distance P to Q	610 nm
Wt, no fuel, no payload	36 500 kg
Max Ldg wt	52 400 kg
Max TOW	63 000 kg
Reserve (unused)	4 000 kg
Fuel for each flight (circuit, take off, etc.)	500 kg
Mean consumption	1 350 kg/hr
Mean G/S P to Q	240 kt
Mean G/S Q to P	280 kt

Give (a) The fuel which must be uplifted at P.

(b) Maximum payload which can be carried from P to Q.

(c) Maximum payload which can be carried from Q to P.

Answer

P to Q: 610 nm @ 240 kt = 2 hr 32 min @ 1 350 kg/hr = 3 420 kg fuel.

Q to P: 610 nm @ 280 kt = 2 hr 10 min @ 1 350 kg/hr = 2 925 kg fuel.

∴ FOB at P	3 420 kg
	2 925 kg
Reserve	4 000 kg
Circuit	1 000 kg
Fuel reqd.	11 345 kg ... (a)

P to Q

Wt, no fuel, no payload	36 500 kg	Max Ldg wt	52 400 kg
FOB	+11 345 kg	Fuel used	3 420 kg
		Circuit	+ 500 kg
Wt, no payload	47 845 kg		
		TOW	56 320 kg
		Wt, no payload	−47 845 kg
		PAYLOAD P to Q	8 475 kg ... (

Q to P

Wt, no fuel, no payload	36 500 kg	Max Ldg wt	52 400 kg
FOB	2 925	Fuel used	2 925 kg
Reserve	4 000	Circuit	+ 500 kg
Circuit	+ 500	TOW	55 825 kg
Wt, no payload	43 925 kg		

∴ TOW	55 825 kg
Wt, no payload	−43 925 kg
PAYLOAD Q to P	11 900 kg ... (c)

11: Point of No Return

PNR is the point beyond which an aircraft cannot go and still return to its departure field within its endurance.

This is entirely a fuel problem, and some reserve for holding or diversion should always be allowed for before setting about the calculation. A PNR is scarcely pertinent on trips over land well served with airfields, though a pilot will often prefer, if his destination and destination alternates are forecast en route to be below limits for his ETA, to return home rather than lob into an airfield where conditions for waiting with a crowd of passengers are miserable, expensive or politically troublesome. But over the oceans and deserts, a PNR is a must; the time to it is noted on the Flight Plan, and the ETA threat put in on departure: it can be amended on the way if forecast winds are diabolically different from actual, or the flight is conducted at a different height or power than planned.

The solution of the problem is invariably found by formula, simply solved on the computer. The distance to the PNR is the distance to be covered back if the aircraft returns, i.e. distance Out = distance Home. The time for this distance at Ground Speed Out plus the time for this distance at Ground Speed Home will equal your endurance time excluding reserves.

If E = total endurance in hours (excluding reserve)

T = Time to PNR in hours

O = G/S Out.

H = G/S Home

R = Distance to the PNR.

Then:

$$E = \frac{R}{O} + \frac{R}{H}$$

$$EOH = R(O + H)$$

$$R = \frac{EOH}{O+H}$$

and since $T = \frac{R}{O}$

$$OT = \frac{EOH}{O+H}$$

$$T = \frac{EH}{O+H}$$

Work in minutes, if you like, as the computer work is eased; and beware of assuming that a wind component Out of +20 must give a Wind Component Home of

−20; at lower G/S, drift is greater, so check the G/S out and home against Track out and home. Having obtained the Time to PNR, the distance can be readily found at G/S out, e.g. endurance 4 hours, excluding 45 min reserve, Track 300(T), W/V 270/40, TAS 200 kt

$\therefore$ G/S Out 164 kt   G/S Home 234 kt

$$T = \frac{240 \times 234}{164 + 234}$$

= 141 min
and 2h 21m at 164 kt = 386 nm

All straightforward and the accuracy of the result can be checked − 2h 21m out + 386 nm at G/S 234 kt or 1h 39m = 4h endurance.

Point of No Return on two or more legs

Weather systems and Traffic Control systems seldom permit a long drag on a Single Track nowadays, and finding the PNR on a route where one or more changes of Track are involved is quite simple, and rational.

Example

Following are route details: ignore climb and descent:−

	Track(T)	Distance	W/V
TAIPEH − KAGOSHIMA	042	606	260/110
KAGOSHIMA − SHIZUOKA	064	417	280/80
SHIZUOKA −TOKYO	011	61	290/50

ATD TAIPEH 1020 GMT
TAS 410 kt
Fuel Consumption 3 000 kg/hr
Reserve (assume unused) 45 min
Fuel on Board 15 000 kg
    Give ETA PNR.
Endurance first for the calculation:
    15 000 kg = 5 hr
Less reserve 45 min
    4h 15m
Now essential Ground Speeds:

	G/S Out	G/S Home
TAIPEH − KAGOSHIMA	491	318
KAGOSHIMA − SHIZUOKA	470	344
SHIZUOKA −TOKYO	396	415

To get rid of the TAIPEH − KAGOSHIMA leg
    at G/S Out 491 kt takes 1h 14m
and if return to TAIPEH from KAGOSHIMA

at G/S Home 318 kt takes 1h 55m

∴ 3h 09m would be required for KAGOSHIMA <u>and back</u>

So endurance from KAGOSHIMA is 1h 06m, and clearly the PNR is on the SHIZUOKA leg.

$$T = \frac{EH}{O + H} = \frac{66 \times 344}{470 + 344} = 28 \text{ min}$$

∴ from TAIPEH, time to PNR is 1h 14m + 28 min = 1h 42m and ETA is 1202 GMT.

And check:

Out to KAGOSHIMA		1h 14m
plus KAGOSHIMA to PNR		28m
	Out	1h 42m

Home 28 min at G/S Out 470 = 220 nm

220 nm Home to KAGOSHIMA at G/S Home 344 kt	38 min
KAGOSHIMA − TAIPEH	1h 55 min
Home	2h 33 m

Total 4h 15m = endurance, leaving 45 min reserve.

The method out and back on Leg 1 could be repeated on further legs until the endurance remaining clearly must resolve the leg on which the PNR is placed.

It is commonplace when a situation arises that an aircraft turns back or diverts, to adjust the power and height, if permissible, in order to economise on fuel; the consumption outwards might be high and carefree but having turned back for any reason at all, it will be very cautious. The PNR in this case becomes a matter of simple algebra, based on the essential knowledge that endurance is known.

e.g.   G/S Out 180 kt, G/S Home 240 kt, consumption out 2 400 kg/hr, consumption home 2 000 kg/hr, fuel available for this calculation 12 500 kg.

Remembering that the distance to the PNR = distance from PNR back home = X nm

$$\text{Then } \left(\frac{X}{180} \times 2\,400\right) + \left(\frac{X}{240} \times 2\,000\right) = 12\,500 \text{ kg}$$

a case of time against consumption out and back.

X, the distance to PNR = 576 nm

and the time to it at G/S Out 180 kt = 3h 12m

A problem of this sort on various legs would be tackled as before, arriving at a turning point with the new fuel remaining, after calculating out <u>and back</u> on previous sectors.

Graphical Solution

Much against our will, we'll put this into the story: it will become part of the Flight Progress graph, another quite unnecessary sheet on any flight, as it presupposes that all aircrew are incapable of understanding anything unless presented to them in pictorial form. It's included in the syllabus in case you find yourself flying for a firm of graph maniacs.

Given: FOB 750 gal, TAS 180 kt, Consumption 95 gal/hr
          Headwind component 25 kt
          Find the PNR, leaving 50 gal in reserve.

Steps: (i)   Endurance for 700 gal at 95 gal/hr = 442 min
          (ii)   Distance OUT for 442 min   = 442 min at G/S 155 kt
                                                   = 1 142 nm
          (iii) Distance HOME for 442 min   = 442 min at G/S 205 kt
                                                   = 1 505 nm
          (iv)   With coordinates fuel and distance, plot these curves.

The point of intersection is the PNR

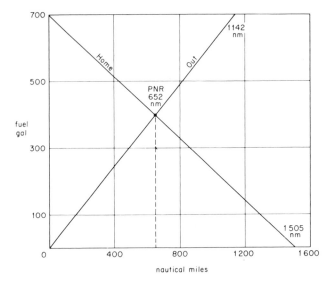

Fig. 11.1

This can be checked correct with the formulae. On the graph, as large a scale as possible should be chosen to ensure an accurate result.

This simple method is of no avail if climb, cruise, descent are involved, or TAS or consumption are variable factors: this lot is part of any decent trip in a decent aeroplane, and the solution by graph becomes quite a sweat.

Proceed as follows:

(i)   Complete the Flight Plan.

(ii)   Plot the Fuel/distance Out, starting with TOC and ending with TOD, reading the stages off the Flight Plan. This is in fact the chart to be used for the Flight progress; as the turning or reporting points are reached, the fuel used so far is entered on the graph, and a comparison with fuel planned is at once visually apparent.

(iii) Draw a line across the graph to represent the fuel available for PNR calculation; where this line meets the fuel coordinate may now be deemed the 'departure point' whither the aircraft is returning having used the PNR fuel.

(iv) From this point, work <u>backwards</u> to TOD and thenceforth in fuel used per sector, until the curves cross. Fig. 11.2.

This is all very clever (apart from being very tedious) as an academic exercise:

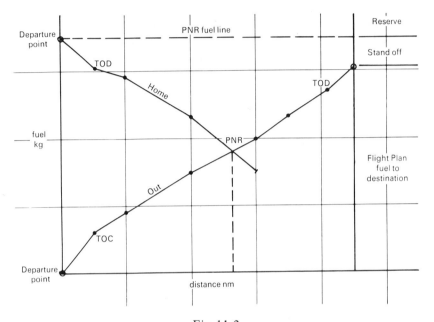

Fig. 11.2

in practice, fuel consumption varies as AUW decreases, or ditto TAS. To do the reverse Flight Plan, the aircraft's weight must be known overhead departure point on return to it: this is found by subtracting the fuel available for PNR from the original TOW, and as the flight home progresses backwards, and the details plotted, a reasonable assumption can be made for the AUW over the obvious PNR leg.

The PNR is usually solved, however, by straightforward methods, and here's a sample to work through, and you should check every figure so that wrinkles can be spotted, and the method acquired.

Using CAP 159, for a flight from A to B assume:
 (i) Distance 1 870 nm
 (ii) TOW 67 000 kg
 (iii) Outward: <u>Climb</u> on Track from 1 000 ft at A to 33 000 ft pressure altitude. Temp dev −3°C, wind component +20. <u>Cruise</u> at 0·75 M_{ind} at 33 000 ft Temp dev +1°C, wind component +45.
 (iv) Homeward: <u>Cruise</u> at 0·75 M_{ind} at 32 000 ft Temp dev −1°C, wind component −40. Use subsidiary table to allow for descent to 1 000 ft over A.
 (v) Fuel available, excluding reserves: 19 800 kg.
Determine the flight time and distance to the PNR.

Here goes!
(i)   Climb Table 31A −3°C Temp dev
         To 33 000 ft for TOW 67 000 kg
              Fuel 2 550 kg   Time 21 min
                  +   500   +   2 min   (T/O to 1 000 ft)
                      3 050 kg   23 min   footnote
              TAS 338 kt, G/S 358 kt for 21 min = 126 nm

(ii)   Cruise Table 31D +1°C Temp dev
         AUW at start of cruise 67 000 kg − 3 050 used on climb
                                          = 63 950 kg
              and fuel remaining   = 16 750 kg (total PNR fuel 19 800
                                          − 3 050 climb)
              Extract TAS 432 kt   ∴ G/S 477 kt
              From 63 950 kg to 58 300 kg AUW
              Consumption is 4 000 kg/hr
         = 5 650 kg to use, takes 1h 25m = 678 nm

We've done just over 800 nm, and used nearly 9 000 kg of fuel, and some watch
must be kept on consumption outward and homeward.
    The next 2 hours on the table we're in gives a consumption of 3 800 kg/hr, but
only 1½ hr on the homebound table of Temp dev −1°C at 32 000 ft
So 1h 30m at 3 800 kg/hr = 5 700 kg
and all is correct whichever way we're going, out or home.
    Fuel used so far: Climb   3 050
                          Level   5 650
                                   5 700

                                  14 400 kg, leaving 5 400 kg in tanks
    This must be homeward, and AUW by then is
              67 000 − 14 400 = 52 600 kg
    Extract from the −1°C table at 32 000 ft, 3 600 kg/hr and the remaining 5 400 kg
will go in 1h 30m
From TOC, the endurance is therefore 4h 25m but in this figure we must balance the
126 nm flown on the climb, and give a thought to the ultimate descent.
    From the Temp dev −1°C Table, TAS is 429 kt
    ∴ G/S 389 kt and 126 nm takes 19 min
    AUW over A on return will be 67 000 kg − 19 800 kg
              = 47 200 kg
    From table, consumption at the end is 3 600 kg/hr
    so 19 min   = 1 140 kg
    The footnote for descent gives 300 kg and 9 min, the fuel being a subtractive
element.
Thus, the outward climb distance has been balanced on return by 840 kg (1 140 − 300),
19 min of time; the extra time on descent being as it were non-fuel consuming. The
cruise endurance is 4h 06m, and the balancing act of that 126 nm can be omitted
from the solution by formula viz:

$$\frac{T}{E} = \frac{H}{O+H} \quad \frac{T}{246} = \frac{389}{477+389} = \frac{246 \times 389}{866}$$
$$= 1h\ 50m$$

Add on the 23 min of climb and the time to the PNR from T/O is 2h 13m resolving itself into a distance from A of 126 + 878 = 1 004 nm.

A Check of this could now be made from the start, and an answer within 200 or 300 kg of the original FOB of 19 800 kg would be satisfactory, as one does avoid half minutes and fuels are rounded off to the 50s.

A question like this at first sight looks best solved graphically; do try it and see.

12: Critical Point

Critical point is the point from which it would take equal time to continue to destination as to return to departure field.

This is not a function of fuel at all whatever: there is a critical point when crossing the road or swimming a river: distance and related G/S are the factors to consider and it is important to bear in mind that it is a Flight Plan problem initially, to prepare for some eventuality like an engine failure when an instant decision must be taken to proceed or return, the quicker being the choice as there is some concern among those present.

Again, the solution is done by simple formula, and the ETA CP entered on the Flight Plan; the same arguments hold as previously as to the trips on which a CP is vital.

Take a straightforward case first

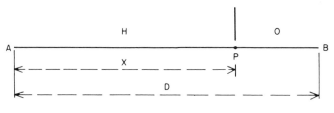

Fig. 12.1

Where D is total distance
        P the Critical Point
        X Distance to CP in nautical miles
        O Ground Speed Out in knots
        H Ground Speed Home in knots
Then by definition:
        P to A at G/S Home = P to B at G/S Out.

i.e.
$$\frac{X}{H} = \frac{D-X}{O}$$
$$OX = H(D - X)$$
$$OX = HD - HX$$
$$OX + HX = HD$$
$$\therefore \quad \frac{DH}{O+H} = X, \text{ the distance to the CP.}$$

Now the CP is bursting with importance when the aircraft is acting up, usually an engine out, not in itself an emergency, but leading towards it if something else happens: an aircraft on 3 engines will not go as fast as on 4, strangely enough, especially when fuel conservation is high priority. An operator, therefore, lays down in the manual an average 3-engined and 2-engined TAS at specified heights; thus, the CP data must be worked using the reduced TAS so that the equal times home and away from the CP are appropriate to the conditions should the exigency occur. In the air, once the CP is passed (and the ETA to it will be calculated at normal G/S, just like a reporting point), the pilot will proceed to his destination. A separate CP at full TAS can be calculated readily, to cope with serious situations like a loose panther in the hold, or a berserk and frothing passenger which affect the safety of the aircraft and its occupants, but not its power. But in a pressurisation failure, for instance, while the power is unaffected, the CP is dependent on a TAS at a new enforced height with implications very similar to the engine failure cases. This, too, calls for a separate CP, not an arduous calculation since the action for the pressurisation failure will be laid down and the optimum height with the appropriate data is set out in the aircraft manual.

There are several pertinent possibilities, then; and bear in mind that they are just that. One or more CPs are noted on the Flight Plan to be referred to as though they are turning points, with their ETA. Once a CP is passed, the pilot's action is clear: if a near-emergency arises, he will aim for the destination airfield. The CP is but a preparation in case of emergency, and if that emergency happens, he has the facts before him at once.

Some samples:
1. Track 240(T), W/V 310/35, TAS 260 kt Distance 530 nm
    $\therefore$ G/S out = 245 kt   G/S home = 270 kt

    $$\text{Distance to CP} = \frac{DH}{O+H}$$

    $$= \frac{530 \times 270}{245 + 270}$$

    $$= 278 \text{ nm}$$

    and time to CP   = 278 at G/S out 245 kt = 1h 08m
Check
    278 at G/S home 270 kt   = 1h 02m
    (530 − 278) at G/S out 245 kt = 1h 02m

2. What is distance to CP en route from DARWIN and MELBOURNE distance 1 728 nm, cruise TAS 425 kt, 3-engine TAS 400 kt, headwind component from CP to MELBOURNE 5 kt, headwind component CP to DARWIN 20 kt?
    $\therefore$ for the CP calculation: G/S out   = 395 kt,
                          G/S home = 380 kt,

    $$\text{Distance to CP} = \frac{DH}{O+H}$$

    $$= \frac{1\,728 \times 380}{395 + 380}$$

    $$= 847 \text{ nm}$$

You check.

The ETA CP can then be found simply from the normal Flight Plan after departure; this type of problem is most frequently used in practice and, despite finding the wind components by inspection, is proved reasonably accurate: with a long trip going fairly to plan until an engine drops out, a pilot who turns back because it happens 5 minutes before the CP cannot be criticised for being dogmatically correct, but his employers and passengers might think him rather lacking in dash and élan.

3.   Now for the several Track CP.

  TAS 200 kt Engine failure TAS 160 kt

  Route

BAGHDAD–BASRA	Track 115(T), Dist 170 nm W/V 180/20
BASRA–KUWAIT	Track 178(T), Dist 110 nm W/V 230/30
KUWAIT–BAHRAIN	Track 129(T), Dist 147 nm W/V 250/15

Find ETA CP if ATD BAGHDAD is 1115.

Draw a freehand diagram, and set in the G/S out and home at reduced TAS.

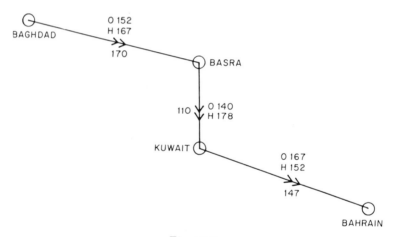

Fig. 12.2

Remember we are concerned in the air, with an engine out, with equal time home and on: we have to get the CP placed on a single leg, balancing the time home with time out.

On BASRA home to BAGHDAD 170 nm at 167 kt gives 1h 01m

Now balance that 1h 01m out on the KUWAIT–BAHRAIN leg,

  147 nm at G/S out 167 kt takes 53 min

There are still 8 min out to take care of, and that will be used up on BASRA–KUWAIT leg.

  8 min at G/S out 140 kt = 19 nm

<u>Thus</u> 1h 01m home balances 1h 01m out, and the CP is on the BASRA–KUWAIT leg, the total distance to be considered

$$110 - 19 \qquad = 91 \text{ nm from BASRA}$$

$$\frac{DH}{O + H} = \frac{91 \times 178}{140 + 178} = 51 \text{ nm from BASRA}$$

<u>ETA CP</u> BAGHDAD–BASRA 170 nm at cruise G/S 192 kt = 53 min
        BASRA – CP 51 nm at cruise G/S 180 kt   = 17 min
        Total time at normal cruise 1h 10m
        ∴ ETA 1225
    You check, that if engine fails at 1225, the time back to BAGHDAD is equal to
the time on to BAHRAIN.

Graphical Solution
Critical Point problems may be solved graphically by plotting two curves, one for the
flight out and the other for the flight home on a distance/time axis graph. The intersection of the two curves indicates CP for the flight, time and distance being read off
the appropriate graph axes.
Example: Speed OUT is less than speed HOME.
              A – B 750 nm wind component – 15 kt
              TAS: 180 kt Full
                    140 kt Reduced
Find CP for both speeds

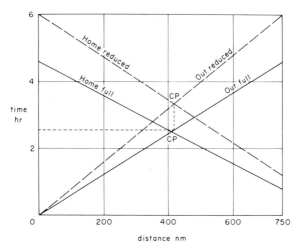

Fig. 12.3

Solution: <u>Full Speed</u>
               G/S Out 165 kt dist 750 nm Time 273 min
               G/S Home 195 kt dist 750 nm Time 231 min
Plot the coordinates distance/time. See Fig. 12.3. CP occurs at distance of 406 nm.
time 2h 28m.
               <u>Reduced Speed</u>
               G/S Out 125 kt dist 750 nm time 360 min
               G/S Home 155 kt dist 750 nm time 290 min
Plot the coordinates distance/time. CP occurs at distance of 415 nm. To find the time to
CP, draw in a line from the point of intersection to the Full Speed out line at a distance of 415 nm and read off the time on the vertical axis of the graph. The time is
2h 31m.

The above solutions may be checked by use of formula.

The accuracy of the result depends on the graph scale.

Example: Speed OUT is more than speed HOME. In this case, the time Home will be greater than time Out. The best way to approach this situation is to find the time out normally, and then work out the distance that would be travelled HOMEWARD in that time. Say the ground speed Out is 195 kt, the ground speed Home is 165 kt, the time taken Out is 231 min and in that time the distance covered on Homeward flight will be 634 nm.

Plot the two curves now and point of intersection is the CP.

13: Flight Planning Re-check

We have laid down the principles and methods of flight planning, but of all the pages a student will be faced with in the professional examinations, speed and accuracy are positively vital in this for satisfying the examiner. So plenty of practice is required in preparation — and there is not much time for cogitation when practically called on while flogging the routes either. Incidentally, polish up the old examination technique; allot the appropriate time to a question that its marks warrant. A 65-mark flight plan in a 2-hour paper demands you leave it after 78 minutes maximum, then on to the 25-mark question for 30 minutes, the 10-mark one for 12 minutes. Unless of course, you are ahead of the game.

CP/PNR figure on every flight plan, and naturally are often asked in the same question in exams, with a few furbelows to add to the examinee's confusion. Here are some marked examples in the hope of avoiding any chewing the pencil in agonised doubt at crucial moments.

First, remember that:

PNR distance <u>out</u> is the same as the distance <u>home.</u> Its position depends on the <u>fuel</u> available for its calculation.

CP <u>time home</u> is the same as the <u>time to</u> destination.

And <u>always</u> draw a diagram, always.

Example 1
An aircraft is to fly from A to B on a Track of 280T distance 959 nm, mean TAS 230 kt. W/V for the first 430 nm is 200/50, and 260/65 for the remaining distance. Fuel on board is 26 500 kg, 3 100 kg to be held in reserve: consumption 3 400 kg/hr. Give the time and distance to:
    (a)   PNR,
    (b)   CP, assuming engine failure at the CP and a reduced TAS of 190 kt.

Answer
(a)   <u>PNR.</u> Draw a diagram first, and insert what is known: a rough direction is adequate, of course.

Fig. 13.1

Tr 280T

TAS 230 kt

$$\text{Endurance} = (26\,500 - 3\,100) \text{ kg @ } 3\,400 \text{ kg/hr}$$
$$= 23\,400 \text{ kg @ } 3\,400 \text{ kg/hr}$$
$$= 6\cdot882 \text{ hr}$$
$$= 6 \text{ hr } 53 \text{ min.}$$

Insert on the diagram the G/S for each leg evolved from the computer.

Treat as two legs, and try to lose A to X in the first place.

A to X <u>out</u> 430 nm @ 217 kt   = 1 hr 59 min

X to A <u>home</u> 430 nm @ 232 kt = 1 hr 51 min

3 hr 50 min

Thus, as the total endurance is 6 hr 53 min, the PNR is beyond X, and we have endurance from X of 3 hr 03 min for the calculation.

<u>Formula</u>

$$T = \frac{EH}{O + H} \quad \text{from X}$$

$$T = \frac{183 \times 291}{291 + 167} \text{ min}$$

$$= \frac{53\,253}{458} \text{ min}$$

$$= 116 \text{ min or } 1 \text{ hr } 56 \text{ min}$$

and at 167 kt = 324 nm from X.

<u>Thus</u> distance to PNR from A is (430 + 324) nm = 754 nm

Time to PNR from A is

	1 hr 59 min	from A to X
+324 nm @ 167 kt	1 hr 56 min	from X to PNR
	3 hr 55 min	from A to PNR

Should the time out from A to X, plus the time home from X to A come to more than the endurance of 6 hr 53 min, then the PNR is on AX, and the second leg is superfluous: the formula could be entered at once. You should be so lucky.

A quick check for correctness:

A to X	1 hr 59 min
X to PNR	1 hr 56 min
PNR–X (324 nm @ 291 kt)	1 hr 07 min
X to A	1 hr 51 min
	6 hr 53 min which is our endurance.

(b)   <u>CP.</u> Repeat the diagram, enter the facts, but this time watch the reduced TAS: equal time from CP to destination and CP to departure field, so the engine has failed, and normal TAS is of no interest whatever to the calculation.

X to A 430 @ 192 kt   2 hr 14 min

X to B 529 @ 128 kt   4 hr 07 min

So the CP is clearly on X to B.

Now X to A takes 2 hr 14 min, and 2 hr 14 min <u>out</u> on XB @ 128 kt = 286 nm.

So from X en route to B of (529 − 286) nm is the area of the CP = 243 nm.

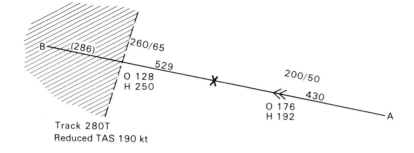

Fig. 13.2

$$\text{Distance to CP from X} = \frac{DH}{O + H}$$

$$= \frac{243 \times 250}{250 + 128} \text{ nm}$$

$$= \frac{60\,750}{378} \text{ nm}$$

$$= 161 \text{ nm}$$

Distance to CP from A = (430 + 161) nm = 591 nm.

Time to CP from A is

At <u>full</u> G/S of 217 kt time to X	1 hr 59 min
+ 161 nm @ 167 kt, from X to CP	58 min
	2 hr 57 min

<u>Check</u>

CP to B = (529 − 161) nm @ 128 kt = 368 nm @ 128 kt = 2 hr 52 min

CP to X = 161 nm @ 250 kt	=	38 min
X to A = 430 nm @ 192 kt	=	2 hr 14 min
		2 hr 52 min

<u>Example 2</u>

This one is severely practical:

Given max TOW weight	61 000 kg
Weight, no fuel, no payload	37 000 kg
TAS	410 kt
Distance	2 250 nm
Consumption	2 800 kg/hr
Reserve (assume unused)	3 200 kg
Hdwd component	40 kt

Determine.

(a) Maximum payload that can be carried.

(b) Time and distance to the CP.

(c) Time and distance to the PNR.

Answer
G/S 370 kt, distance 2 250 nm.
∴ Time to destination 6 hr 05 min
At 2 800 kg/hr, fuel used = 17 035 kg, rounded off.

Empty wt	37 000 kg	Max TOW	61 000 kg
Fuel	17 035 kg	Wt, no payload	57 235 kg
Reserve	3 200 kg	PAYLOAD	3 765 kg . . . (a)
Wt, no payload	57 235 kg		

CP.
G/S out, 370 kt; G/S home, 450 kt.

$$\text{Distance to CP} = \frac{DH}{O + H}$$

$$= \frac{2\,250 \times 450}{370 + 450} \text{ nm}$$

$$= \frac{1\,012\,500}{820} \text{ nm}$$

$$= 1\,235 \text{ nm} \quad \ldots \text{(b)}$$

And time is 1 235 nm @ G/S 370 kt = 3 hr 22 min . . . (b)
Check
1 235 nm @ 450 kt = 2 hr 45 min
1 015 nm @ 370 kt = 2 hr 45 min.
PNR.

$$T = \frac{EH}{O + H}$$

$$= \frac{365 \times 450}{370 + 450} \text{ min}$$

$$= \frac{164\,250}{820} \text{ min}$$

$$T = 3 \text{ hr } 20 \text{ min} \quad \ldots \text{(c)}$$

And distance is 3 hr 20 min @ 370 kt = 1 233 nm   . . . (c)
Check

Out	3 hr 20 min
Home 1 233 nm @ 450 kt	2 hr 45 min
Endurance	6 hr 05 min

Example 3
This is a PNR involving a return to base on 3 engines, and on several Tracks, practical
enough, but there are pitfalls easily fallen into, if you are rushed for time.
    An a/c is to fly from F to G via K and M; the data is as follows:

Stage	Wind component (kt)	Distance (nm)
F to K	+20	400
K to M	+15	630
M to G	+25	605

Mean TAS	500 kt
Mean TAS (3 engines)	435 kt
Mean fuel consumption (4 engines)	5 300 kg/hr
Mean fuel consumption (3 engines)	4 100 kg/hr
Fuel on board (inc. Reserve, 5500 kg, assume unused)	30 000 kg

Calculate the time and distance to the PNR from departure F, the return flight to F to be made on 3 engines.

Answer

Draw a diagram first and put the data on it; the G/S out and home are inserted when found as below.

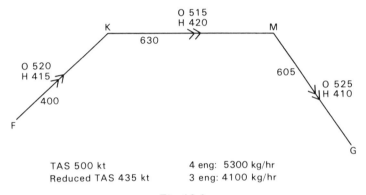

Fig. 13.3

Fuel available is (30 000 − 5 500) kg = 24 500 kg.

Only the return flight is to be made on 3 engines, so G/S out is on 4 engines, G/S home is on 3 engines.

Do the 4 engine G/S first, F to K for example (500 + 20) kt = 520 kt.
The G/S home on 3 engines will be at the opposite sign of the wind component:
We are stating the obvious, but would you believe . . .?
Start at F to K, out and home:

Out   400 nm @ 520 kt = 46 min @ 5 300 kg/hr = 4 050 kg used
Home 400 nm @ 415 kt = 58 min @ 4 100 kg/hr = 3 950 kg used

∴ Fuel used   8 000 kg

Still well in hand, so repeat on K to M:
Out   630 nm @ 515 kt = 1 hr 13 min @ 5 300 kg/hr = 6 450 kg used
Home 630 nm @ 420 kt = 1 hr 30 min @ 4 100 kg/hr = 6 150 kg used

∴ Fuel used   12 600 kg

Fuel used for the calculation so far is 20 600 kg, so the fuel available at M is 24 500 − 20 600 = 3 900 kg.
   As fuel consumption is different on the out and home legs, the formula is no use, and we go into the maths bit, with x = distance to the PNR from M

Total fuel at M for PNR $= \left(\dfrac{\text{dist}}{\text{G/S out}} \times \text{fuel consumption on 4 engines} \right)$

$$+ \left(\dfrac{\text{dist}}{\text{G/S home}} \times \text{fuel consumption on 3 engines} \right)$$

$$3\,900 = \left(\dfrac{x}{525} \times 5\,300 \right) + \left(\dfrac{x}{410} \times 4\,100 \right)$$

$$3\,900 = 101x + 10x$$

$$\therefore x = 194 \text{ nm}$$

Distance to PNR from M is 194 nm.
We require time and distance to the PNR from F:

F to K   400 nm @ 520 kt =   46 min
K to M   630 nm @ 515 kt = 1 hr 13 min
M to PNR 194 nm @ 525 kt =   22 min

Distance 1 224 nm   2 hr 21 min

Time 2 hr 21 min and distance 1 224 nm to the PNR from F.
Check
Out

F to K	4 050 kg
K to M	6 450 kg
M to PNR 22 min @ 5 300 kg/hr	1 950 kg
Home	
PNR to M: 194 nm @ 410 kt = $28\frac{1}{2}$ min @ 4 100 kg/hr	1 950 kg
M to K	6 150 kg
K to F	3 950 kg
Fuel available for PNR	24 500 kg

Example 4
This is quite a nasty one.
On a trip from P to R via Q, an a/c is ordered in the event of turning back to proceed to its alternate Y via Q. TAS on 4 engines is 500 kt, on 3 engines is 420 kt.

Stage	Wind component (kt)	Distance (nm)
P to Q	−25	565
Q to R	−45	900
Q to Y	+30	240

(a)   If the return from CP is made on 3 engines, give the time and distance from P to the CP between R and Y.

(b)   FOB 38 000 kg, consumption 6 300 kg/hr, reserve (assume unused) 6 500 kg, and the whole flight is made on 4 engines, what is the distance from P to PNR to Y?

Answer
(a)   CP.   Draw the picture, and insert what we can.

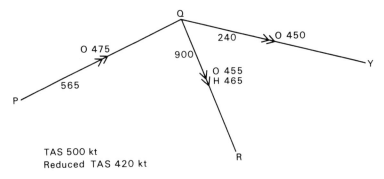

Fig. 13.4

We need to find the equal time to carry on from the CP to R on 4 engines and the return from the CP to Y on 3 engines.
Now QY on 3 engines = 240 nm @ 450 kt = 32 min.
Apply this 32 min <u>out</u> on QR @ 455 kt = 242 nm.
We are left with (900 − 242) nm = 658 nm on QR for the CP

$$\text{Distance of the CP from Q} = \frac{DH}{O + H}$$

$$= \frac{658 \times 465}{455 + 465} \, nm$$

$$= \frac{305\,970}{920} \, nm$$

$$= 333 \, nm$$

Distance from P to Q	565 nm
Distance from Q to CP on QR	333 nm
	898 nm . . . (a)

Time P to Q: 565 nm @ 475 kt	1 hr 12 min
Time Q to CP: 333 nm @ 455 kt	+ 44 min
	1 hr 56 min . . . (a)

Check
333 nm home to Q at 465 kt	43 min
Q to Y	+ 32 min
	1 hr 15 min

On QR, (900 − 333) nm = 567 nm at 455 kt = 1 hr 15 min.
(b)   <u>PNR.</u>   It is advisable for clarity to re-draw the sketch, as it is all on 4 engines.
Consumption is constant, so there is no need to sweat out each leg.

FOB	38 000 kg
Reserve	6 500 kg
Fuel available	31 500 kg @ 6 300 kg/hr = 5 hr.

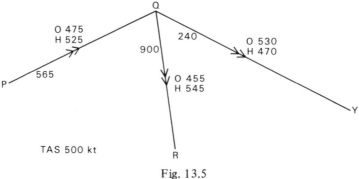

Fig. 13.5

PQ, 565 nm @ 475 kt = 1 hr 13 min

∴ Endurance at Q = 3 hr 47 min.

The PNR is thus on QR for sure.

QY, 240 nm @ 530 kt = 27 min.

Endurance left is 3 hr 20 min.

$$T = \frac{EH}{O + H}$$

$$T = \frac{200 \times 545}{455 + 545}$$

$$= \frac{109\,000}{1\,000} \text{ min}$$

$$= 1 \text{ hr } 49 \text{ min, from Q to PNR}$$

and distance =   829 nm

Add P to Q =   565 nm

1 394 nm from P   ... (b)

Check

P to Q	1 hr 13 min	PNR to Q, 829 nm @ 545 kt	1 hr 31 min
Q to PNR	1 hr 49 min	Q to Y	27 min
	3 hr 02 min		1 hr 58 min
Total	3 hr 02 min		
	1 hr 58 min		
	5 hr 00 min		

Example 5

There is a lot to be said for working out a full flight plan, completing it with a CP and PNR: after all, that is what would happen on the routes when you are forced to land at a field not manned by your own company's personnel.

Let us take one step-by-step with the trimmings left out:

A flight is to be made from A to D at cruise Mach 0·75: FOB 23 000 kg, reserve fuel (assume unused) 4 000 kg. Ignore descent.

FLIGHT PLAN

STAGE From	STAGE To	Temp. °C	* Flight Level	* Temp. Dev. °C	* WIND Direction	* WIND Speed kt	* Track °(T)	Drift	Heading °(T)	TAS kt	Wind comp. kt	G/S kt	* Distance nm	Time min	* Fuel flow kg/hr	Fuel required kg
A	B	-42	330	+ 9	230	60	290	7S	283	445	-35	410	430	63	4 000	4 200
B	C	-46	330	+ 5	250	70	303	8S	295	440	-49	391	365	56	3 700	3 450
C	D	-53	330	- 2	260	50	312	5S	307	434	-34	400	386	58	3 550	3 430
D	C	-50	310	- 3	270	40	132	3P	135	437	+31	468	386	49½	3 650	3 000
C	B	-42	310	+ 5	240	60	123	7P	130	445	+25	470	365	46½	3 750	2 900
B	A	-36	310	+11	220	50	110	6P	116	450	+15	465	430	55½	3 700	3 410

Complete the flight plan and calculate

     (a)   time and distance for PNR to A

     (b)   time and distance for CP between A and D.

In our print of the flight plan, the data given has the column marked with an asterisk.

1. Evolve the temperature at FL from the temperature deviation column.

Standard temperature at FL 330 is $-51°C$

    (33 000 ft @ 2°C per 1 000 ft = $-66°C$

                Standard at sea level = $\underline{+15°C}$

                                     $-51°C$)

                    $\therefore$ A to B = -42

                         B to C = -46

                         C to D = -53

Fill in the return temperature details.

2. Evolve TAS from Mach 0·75 from computer.

Mach index in Airspeed window v ambient temperature and read speed of sound on outer scale against 1 on the inner.

Do you agree consecutively 593, 587, 579, 583, 593, 600?

Then $\dfrac{TAS}{Sof\ S}$ = Mach 0·75, or simply 593 on outer scale against 10 on inner,

and read off 445 on outer against 0·75 on inner, and so on, and the TAS is as shown on the flight plan.

3. Complete the flight plan. We have 19 000 kg usable fuel, adequate for A to D and some suitable alternate.

Now for the PNR.

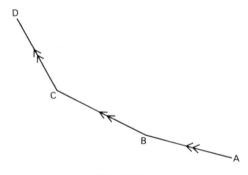

Fig. 13.6

The diagram is not quite so necessary, but is still a useful guide: the PNR is best worked out in terms of <u>fuel</u> rather than time, direct from the Flight Plan form.

                A to B out   4 200 kg

                B to A home $\underline{3\ 410\ kg}$

                                  $\underline{7\ 610\ kg}$

So with available fuel for the trip 19 000 kg, we are left with 11 390 kg at B for PNR purposes.

B to C out	3 450 kg
C to B home	2 900 kg
	6 350 kg

∴ at C, fuel left is (11 390 − 6 350) kg = 5 040 kg and PNR is on CD.
G/S out is 400 kt, at consumption 3 550 kg/hr
G/S home is 468 kt, at consumption 3 650 kg/hr

$$5\,040 = \left(\frac{X}{400} \times 3\,550\right) + \left(\frac{X}{468} \times 3\,650\right)$$

where X is the distance to PNR from C,

$$5\,040 = 8{\cdot}875X + 7{\cdot}8X$$
$$\therefore \quad X = 302 \text{ nm}$$

which at G/S 400 kt is 45 min.
Distance and time to PNR from A

A to B	430 nm	1 hr 03 min
B to C	365 nm	56 min
C to PNR	302 nm	45 min
	1 097 nm	2 hr 44 min ... (a)

Check
Out:

	4 200 kg
	3 450 kg
C to PNR @ 3 550 kg/hr	2 660 kg
	10 310 kg

Home:
PNR to C is 302 nm @ 468 kt = 39 min

39 min @ 3 650 kg/hr	2 370 kg
	2 900 kg
	3 410 kg
	8 680 kg

Total fuel (10 310 + 8 680) kg = 18 990 kg, and we have lost just about 10 seconds of fuel consumption.
CP

B to A takes $55\frac{1}{2}$ min.
Balance with C to D: $55\frac{1}{2}$ min at G/S 400 kt = 370 nm.
On CD, left with 16 nm @ 400 kt = $02\frac{1}{2}$ min.
Balance on CB home: $02\frac{1}{2}$ min @ 470 kt = 20 nm.
∴ left on BC with 345 nm.

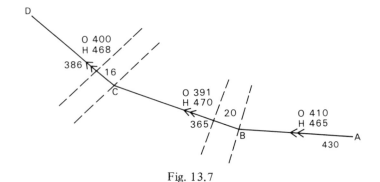

Fig. 13.7

$$\text{Distance to CP} = \frac{DH}{O + H}$$

$$= \frac{345 \times 470}{391 + 470} \text{ nm}$$

$$= \frac{162\,150}{861} \text{ nm}$$

$$= 188 \text{ nm}$$

∴ CP is (188 + 20) nm from B   208 nm
             A to B   430 nm

                    638 nm   ... (b)

and <u>time:</u>   A to B   1 hr 03 min
             B to CP   32 min

                 1 hr 35 min   ... (b)

<u>Check</u>
CP to B (208 nm @ 470 kt) $26\frac{1}{2}$ min
B to A $55\frac{1}{2}$ min

                        1 hr 22   min

CP to C (157 nm @ 391 kt)   24   min
C to D   58   min

                        1 hr 22   min

Now a few worked examples which hurl you into the tables.

An aircraft is at FL 350 over aerodrome B: its weight is 123 000 kg, and it is cruising at Mach 0·86, mean headwind component 60 kt, temperature deviation −7°C. Fuel on board excluding reserves is 21 000 kg.

What is the range of the aircraft which will permit it to return to overhead B at the same FL? (Use Table 33C)

Fig. 13.8

Table 33C in the $-10°C$ to $-1°C$ temperature deviation set, with a lucky 123 000 kg all up weight gives

Fuel flow   6 700 for 1st hour ∴ 14 300 kg left
            6 500 for 2nd hour ∴ 7 800 kg left
            6 200 for 3rd hour ∴ 1 600 kg left
            ─────
            19 400 in 3 hours
            ─────

and 1 600 kg at the 4th hour flow of 6 000 kg/hr will be used in 16 minutes. So Endurance is 3 hr 16 min.

TAS is 475K, so O and H can be inserted on diagram, and the formula entered.

$$T = \frac{EH}{O + H}$$

$$= \frac{196 \times 535}{415 + 535} \text{ min}$$

$$= \frac{104\,860}{950} \text{ min}$$

$$= 110 \text{ min or } 1 \text{ hr } 50 \text{ min}$$

and at 415 kt, the distance out is 760 nm.
A quick check will verify this.

We must try the other tables, so there follows a descent and hold job: for the holding, use Table 33D.

An aircraft is over its destination field (elevation 3 000 ft) at 30 000 ft, weight 88 000 kg, temperature deviation $-3°C$. The aircraft is instructed to hold at FL 140. Allowing fuel for circuit and landing from 1 000 ft of 1 000 kg, how long can it hold if fuel to be used before landing must not exceed 5 000 kg?

From the descent table (Table 33E), the descent from FL 300 to FL 40 (1 000 ft over the field) takes 12 min and uses 500 kg. Add to this the circuit and landing fuel of 1 000 kg, then we have (5 000 − 1 500) kg, 3 500 kg for holding.

In Table 33D, read off against Pressure Height and Temp. dev. the fuel flow 6 600 kg/hr. But watch the footnote: $1\frac{1}{2}\%$ reduction in flow for every 5 000 kg in mean weight below 100 000 kg.

The hold will start at 87 700 kg AUW, since the descent from FL 300 to FL 140 uses 300 kg, a simple subtraction in Table 33E; and the hold will use 3 500 kg, so the mean weight will be (87 700 − 1 750) kg = 85 950 kg, call it 86 000 kg.

A decrease of 14 000 kg in weight = 4·2%, and 4·2% of 6 600 kg is 277 kg (we are keeping up the pedantic work). ∴ flow is 6 320 kg, rounding off the digits and 3 500 kg @ 6 320 kg/hr = 33 min, holding.

Keep going!

An aircraft diverts from 1 000 ft overhead its destination aerodrome (elevation 4 000 ft) to its alternate (elevation 2 700 ft). Weight is 75 000 kg, distance is 515 nm, mean wind component −45 kt.

The diversion is made at FL 320, temp. dev. −8°C.

    (a)   What fuel is required to overhead alternate (Table 33G)?

    (b)   Give mean TAS for climb from FL 200 to FL 320, temp. dev. −6°C (Table 33B).

(a) A spot of interpolation in Table 33G; against ground distances 510 nm and 520 nm, and in headwind component columns 40 and 50.

> 515 nm at −50 reads 7 485 kg, 85 min at FL 420.
> 515 nm at −40 reads 7 355 kg, 83 min at FL 420.
> So at −45, use 7 420 kg, 84 min at FL 420.

Now for the corrections:

1.	Start diversion at 5 000 ft	−300 kg
3.	End diversion at 3 700 ft	Nil

3.   Start diversion at 75 000 kg
     so subtract 1% of fuel for each 1 500 kg below 90 000 kg
     10% of 7 420 kg   −740 kg

4.   Cruise at FL 320 for 84 min.
    If at FL 350, +240 kg for 84 min.
    If at FL 300, +1 020 kg for 84 min.
    $\therefore$ 84 min at FL 320 = 1 020 − ($\frac{2}{3}$ × 780) = +700 kg

                                     −340 kg

    $\therefore$ fuel required 7 080 kg   . . . (a)

(b) Table 33B.

Cross from 32 Top of climb height to the 20 000 ft curve, down to the reference line, then UP to −6°C temp. dev. Read 412 kg?

A swinger of the following sort turns up about once a year in the ATPL, worth a packet; we have already done one of these, but not with an entrance into the tables, nor calling for some inspired guesswork. Use Tables 34C and 34G as appropriate.

An aircraft is to fly from PETALING to GLINKA, via KARVEL. Should an engine fail after overlying KARVEL, the return must be made to the alternate QUONTEK, via KARVEL.

    The route details are as follows:

SECTOR	Distance (nm)	F/L	Wind Component (kt)	Temp. (°C)
PETALING to KARVEL	870	250	−20	−18
KARVEL to GLINKA	640	260	−30	−23
GLINKA to KARVEL	640	250	+30	−22
KARVEL to QUONTEK	700	260	−25	−23

Weight at start 280 000 kg, fuel available excluding reserves 61 000 kg: ignore climb and descent.

If an engine fails after KARVEL, how far can it travel towards GLINKA before turning for QUONTEK as directed?

Diagram first, and do not move without consulting it and the table of route details.

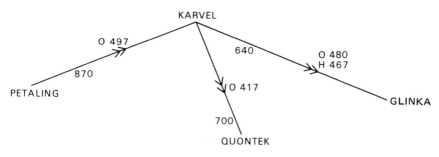

Fig. 13.9

PET. to KARV.:

Table 34C. Temp. dev. is SA + 17, isn't it?

For FL 250, read TAS 517 kt.

G/S is 497 kt, time 1 hr 45 min.

Fuel. 1st hour	13 900 kg
45 min at 13 700 kg/hr	10 275 kg
Fuel used to KARV.	24 175 kg
Weight at start	280 000 kg
Fuel used to KARV.	24 175 kg
Weight at KARV. is	255 825 kg

with fuel (61 000 − 24 175) kg = 36 825 kg remaining.

KARV. to QUONT:

We must know how much fuel is required for this sector before setting off for GLINKA. This is Table 34G, 3-engine cruise, as this sector is only of interest if we have got one engine out. Temp. dev. is +14°C, so in this table, having done some flying to and back on the KARV. to GLINK. leg, some reasonable assumption of weight must be made. Read between 245 000 kg and 235 000 kg, perhaps (we are not exactly loaded, with fuel of 36 825 kg, it is only 2 hours odd in normal flight, rough check).

So TAS, 442 kt ∴ G/S, 417. Time 1 hr 40 min.

Fuel. 1st hour	10 400 kg
40 min at 10 000 kg/hr	6 660 kg
	17 060 kg

∴ Fuel for PNR from KARVEL en route GLINKA is

$$36\,825 \text{ kg} - 17\,060 \text{ kg} = 19\,765 \text{ kg.}$$

And the weight at KARV. is 255 825 kg, don't forget.

KARV. to GLINK.:
So out, SA + 14°C, Table 34C, TAS 510
∴ G/S 480, fuel flow 12 900 kg/hr.
GLINK. to KARV.:
The home leg, 3 engines, Table 34G, SA + 13°C, we are at FL 250, you know.
Use the 245 000 kg to 235 000 kg weight column, TAS 437 kt. ∴ G/S 467 kt, fuel flow 10 500 kg/hr.
The old formula, X = distance in nm.

$$19\,765 = \left(\frac{X}{480} \times 12\,900\right) + \left(\frac{X}{467} \times 10\,500\right)$$

$$= 27X + 22X$$

$$19\,765 = 49X$$

$$X = 403 \text{ nm}$$

which is actually the answer required.

14: PNR Theorems

1. To prove that if fuel available is just sufficient to reach the destination both CP and PNR are in the same position.

E x O is the total distance the a/c can travel out within its endurance.

If endurance is only sufficient to reach its destination, then

$$E \times O = D; \quad \text{and CP is } \frac{DH}{O + H}$$

$$\therefore \frac{EOH}{O + H} = \frac{DH}{O + H}$$

2. To prove that the distance to PNR remains unchanged if the wind component is reversed.

Let TAS of the aircraft be T knots and the wind component, W kt. Then, with headwind, the ground speed Out $= (T - W)$ kt, and

ground speed Home $= (T + W)$ kt.

Distance to PNR with headwind component

$$= \frac{EOH}{O + H} = \frac{E \times (T - W)(T + W)}{(T - W) + (T + W)}$$

$$= \frac{E(T^2 - W^2)}{2T}$$

Distance to PNR with tailwind component

$$= \frac{EOH}{O + H} = \frac{E \times (T + W)(T - W)}{(T + W) + (T - W)}$$

$$= \frac{E(T^2 - W^2)}{2T}$$

$$(\text{Note: with tail wind } O = T + W \text{ and}$$
$$H = T - W)$$

Thus, the distance remains unchanged.

3. To prove that in zero wind condition the distance to PNR is the maximum distance.

When wind is zero, the Distance to PNR formula may be rewritten

$$\frac{EOH}{O + H} = \frac{E \times T \times T}{T + T}$$

where T is the TAS and in zero wind conditions $O = H = T$.

$$= \frac{E \times T^2}{2T}$$

$$= \frac{ET}{2} \quad \ldots\ldots \quad \ldots\ldots \quad \ldots\ldots \quad \ldots\ldots \quad 1.$$

We note, from above theorem (no. 2) that distance to PNR with head or tail component is given in formula

$$\frac{E(T^2 - W^2)}{2T}$$ ....   2.

The value of formula 1 is higher than formula 2, or, the distance to PNR is maximum when wind is zero. You check.

4.   To prove that the distance to PNR is reduced to zero distance when wind component equals TAS.

Distance to PNR in terms of TAS

$= \dfrac{E(T^2 - W^2)}{2T}$ irrespective of whether W is head or tail component.

When W = T, the formula becomes —

$$\frac{E \times zero}{2T}$$

$$= Zero$$

5.   To prove that with no wind, the CP is midway between departure and destination.

Distance to CP $= \dfrac{DH}{O + H}$

With no wind, H = O = T and the formula becomes

Distance $= \dfrac{D \times T}{2T}$

$= \dfrac{D}{2}$

or, midway.

6.   To prove that the CP is closer to destination (as against departure aerodrome) when there is head wind component.

Dist $= \dfrac{DH}{O + H}$; with headwind, H = T + W. Rewriting the formula,

Dist $= \dfrac{D(T + W)}{2T}$

$= \dfrac{D}{2} \times \dfrac{(T + W)}{T}$ which is greater than $\dfrac{D}{2}$

Therefore, CP is nearer destination.

7.   To prove that with tail wind CP is closer to the departure.

Dist to CP $= \dfrac{D}{2} \times \left(\dfrac{T - W}{T} \right)$

which is less than $\dfrac{D}{2}$

8.   To prove that a reduction in TAS with head wind component results in increase of distance to CP.

Distance to CP at normal TAS with head wind

$= \dfrac{D}{2} \times \dfrac{T + W}{T}$ or, $\dfrac{D}{2} \left(1 + \dfrac{W}{T} \right)$

Let the TAS T be reduced by X knots; then $\dfrac{DH}{O + H}$

$$= \frac{D \times (T - X + W)}{(T - X - W) + (T - X + W)}$$

$$= \frac{D(T - X + W)}{2T - 2X}$$

$$= \frac{D}{2} \left(\frac{T - X + W}{T - X} \right)$$

$$= \frac{D}{2} \left(1 + \frac{W}{T - X} \right) \text{ which is greater than } \frac{D}{2} \left(1 + \frac{W}{T} \right)$$

(Note: This is because factor $\frac{W}{T - X}$ is greater than factor $\frac{W}{T}$ in that in the first factor you are dividing W by something less than T.)

Therefore, the distance to CP is increased.

It can similarly be proved that the distance decreases with tail wind component.

APPENDICES

1: Glossary of Abbreviations

a/c	aircraft
A/D	aerodrome
ADF	automatic direction finding equipment
ADIZ	air defence identification zone
ADR	advisory route
agl	above ground level
A/H	alter heading
alt or Alt	altitude
amsl	above mean sea level
ASI	airspeed indicator
ASR	Altimeter Setting Region
ATA	actual time of arrival
ATCC	Air Traffic Control Centre
ATD	actual time of departure
ATZ	Air Traffic Control zone
AUW	all-up weight
Brg	Bearing
BS	Broadcasting station
°C	degrees Celsius, hitherto called Centigrade
°(C)	degrees Compass
CA	conversion angle
CAA	Civil Aviation Authority
CAVOK	weather fine and clear
ch lat	change of latitude
ch long	change of longitude
CL	chart length
cm	centimetre(s)
C of G	centre of gravity
Comp	component
CP	critical point
C/S or c/s	call sign
CTR	control zone
Dev	deviation
DF	direction finding
DGI	directional gyro indicator
dist	distance
DME	distance measuring equipment
DR	dead reckoning

EAT	expected approach time
ETA	estimated time of arrival
ETD	estimated time of departure
ETW	empty tank weight
FIR	Flight Information Region
FIS	Flight Information Service
FL	flight level
FOB	fuel on board
ft	feet
ft/min	feet per minute
°(G)	degrees Grid
G/C	Great circle
GCA	Ground Controlled Approach
GD	Greenwich date
GMT	Greenwich Mean Time
Griv	grivation
G/S	ground speed
H24	operates 24 hours daily
Hdg	Heading
HF	High frequency
HJ	daylight hours
h m s	hours minutes seconds
hr(s)	hour(s)
ht	height
Hz	Hertz (or) cycles per second
IAS	indicated airspeed
IFR	instrument flight rules
ILS	instrument landing system
IMC	instrument meteorological conditions
in	inch
ISA	International Standard atmosphere
Item A	the fuel from departure point to destination only
kg	kilogram(s)
kg/hr	kilograms per hour
kHz	kilohertz, or kilocycles per hour
km/hr	kilometres per hour
kt	knot(s)
Lat	Latitude
Ldg wt	landing weight
LD	Local Date; also landing distance
LF	Low frequency
LMT	Local Mean Time
Long	Longitude
LRC	Long Range Cruise
M	Mach
°(M)	degrees Magnetic
Mb/mb	millibar(s)

M–F	operates Mon. to Friday only
MF	Medium frequency
MHz	megahertz, or megacycles per second
min	minute(s)
M_{ind}	indicated Mach number
mm	millimetre(s)
MN	Mach number, Magnetic north
mph	statute miles per hour
msl	mean sea level
M/R	Moonrise
M/S	Moonset
NDB	non-directional radio beacon
NH	Northern hemisphere
NM/nm	nautical mile(s)
NP	North Pole
OM	outer marker
O/R	on request
PAR	Precision Approach Radar
PE	pressure error
P/L	position line
PNR	point of no return
posn	position
PP	pinpoint
PPO	prior permission only
Press Alt	pressure altitude
QDM, QDR, QNH, QTE	defined in the text
RAS	rectified airspeed
Rel	relative
R/L	Rhumb line
RMI	radio magnetic indicator
R/W	Runway
Rx	Receiver
SA	standard atmosphere
sg	specific gravity
SH	Southern hemisphere
S/H	set heading
sm	statute mile(s)
SP	South Pole
S/R	Sunrise
SRA	special rules area
SRZ	special rules zone
S/S	Sunset
SSR	Secondary Surveillance Radar
ST	Standard Time
Stn	Station
°(T)	degrees True
TAS	True airspeed

Temp	temperature
TMA	terminal control area
TMG	Track made good
TN	True North
T/O	take-off
TOC	top of climb
TOD	Top of descent, also take-off distance
TOW	take-off weight
Tr	Track
TVOR	terminal VHF omni-directional range
Tx	transmitter
UKAP	United Kingdom Aeronautical Information Publication, known as the UK Air Pilot
UHF	Ultra high frequency
u/s	unserviceable
Var	variation
VDF	VHF direction finding
VFR	visual flight rules
VHF	very high frequency
vis	visibility
VMC	visual meteorological conditions
V_{NE}	never exceed speed
V_{NO}	normal speed
VOR	VHF omni-directional range
W/D	wind direction
Wind comp	wind component
W/E	wind effect
W/S	wind speed
wt	weight
W/V	wind velocity

2: Conversion Factors

Imp gal	to	litres	multiply by 4·546
litres		Imp gal	0·22
Imp gal		US gal	1·205
US gal		Imp gal	0·83
gal		cubic ft	0·161
cubic ft		gal	6·25
lb/sq in		kg/cm^2	0·07
lb		kg	0·454
kg		lb	2·205
ft		metres	0·3048
metres		ft	3·2808
sm		nm	0·8684
nm		sm	1·1515
sm		km	1·609
km		sm	0·621
nm		km	1·852
km		nm	0·54
in		mb	33·86
mb		in	0·0295
°C		°F	use formula $(°C \times \frac{9}{5}) + 32$
°F		°C	use formula $(°F - 32) \times \frac{5}{9}$

3: Navigation Equipment, Charts, etc.

Plotting gear: can be bought at a number of shops providing for draughtsmen, but is best obtained from those specialising in airmen's requirements:

Airtour International, at Elstree Aerodrome, Herts has a large stock; they have other branches.

Kay's of Ealing, 8 Bond Street, Ealing, W5.

Dividers: buy the compass-divider type (those vast contraptions that look like instruments for getting the tops off bottles of pickles are strictly for the yachties).

Protractor: Douglas, with the N in red.

Parallel Rules: if you like this sort of thing.

Rule: a 20″ one is a good investment, with inches, tenths, and centimetres, but avoid any map scale on it.

Computer: there are numerous types, some at very fancy prices;

avoid movable wind-arms, make sure it goes up to high speeds and has all the refinements like sg, Mach, etc. on the circular slide rule.

Maps and charts: obtainable from

Edward Stanford Ltd, 12–14 Long Acre, London, WC2.

Airtour International, as above.

International Aeradio Ltd, Hayes Road, Southall, Middlesex.

The latest type Lambert 1:1 000 000 instructional plotting chart as used in the CPL examination is now available, and is really essential for the practice work in this book.

The various charts for the ATPL examination are ICAO plotting Mercator:

LON–GIB–MALTA

SHANNON–KRAKOW–STOCKHOLM

Aerad charts: the useful one for this book is any fairly recent Eur1/2.

Aeronautical Information Circulars are obtainable free from Aeronautical Information Service, Tolcarne Drive, Pinner, Middlesex, HA5 2DU.

The circular on aviation charts is a handy reference, and it has a list of chart symbols.

Specimen examination papers for both CPL and ATPL, Data Sheets for Flight Planning, are all from

CAA, Greville House, 37 Gratton Road, Cheltenham.

No prices have been suggested for any of the above — what's the use?

Index

Index